REAL DEVOTION

Discovering the Whys Behind the Whats of the Gospel

D. ALEXANDER RODRIGUEZ

Foreword by Eli and Mary Gautreaux

Real Devotion:
Discovering the Whys Behind the Whats of the Gospel
By D. Alexander Rodriguez

Copyright © May 2021
Wisdom House Publishing
2003 Stapleton Dr., Friendswood, TX 77546

www.WisdomHousePubs.com
281.352.6540

All rights reserved. No part of this book may be reproduced, stored in a retrieval system or transmitted, in any form or by any means, electronic, photocopying, recording, or otherwise, without written permission of the publisher.

Unless otherwise noted, all Scripture references are from the New King James Version of the Holy Bible. Published 1987 by Thomas Nelson Publishers. Used by permission.

Cover design: Jay Loucks
ISBN: 978-0-578-90979-0
Printed in the United States of America

To Eli and Mary, Eli and Jason, who taught us
we can change the world from Huntsville, Texas.

ACKNOWLEDGMENTS

Thank you to Harvey Herman. A few years back, you dropped a few books written by Chi Alphans that could be counted on one hand, and said we needed more. That was motivation.

Thank you to Dick Brogden. A few years back, you told a group of us visiting the Middle East that if we wrote books, we would make disciples posthumously. That was inspiration.

And thank you to Nathan Cole. A few years back you heard the reading of Chapter 1, and told me the National Chi Alpha Ministry Center would do whatever it could to enable me to write. That was encouraging.

Thank you to Andrew Romano, Ty Cannady, Taylor Cruz, and the Sunday School class of Central Assembly of God for letting me practice the content of this book with you as discipleship content. It was an absolute pleasure!

Thank you again to Eli and Mary Gautreaux, for your gracious blessing in allowing me to write this book on convictions learned at Sam Houston. I hope I have done these truisms justice.

And to my lovely wife, Abby, and my dream, Wesley Kate, I am forever grateful for you both.

CONTENTS

FOREWORD
7

INTRODUCTION
9

PART I
Foundational Principles:
Unfamiliar Whys Behind Familiar Beliefs
17

CHAPTER ONE
Motive is, "Why Do You Do the Things You Do,
and Who Do You Do Them For?"
19

CHAPTER TWO
God's Laws Are Not Motivations for Obedience,
But Descriptions of Reality from an Infinite Perspective
27

CHAPTER THREE
Sin is Not the Breaking of an Impersonal Law,
But the Personal Heart of God
35

CHAPTER FOUR
God Has a Right to Our Lives,
Not Because of What He Does, But Who He Is
45

CHAPTER FIVE
Love Finds a Need and Meets It
55

PART II:
Faithful Practices:
Unfamiliar Whys Behind Familiar Behaviors
65

CHAPTER SIX
Humility is a Sober Sense of Reality
67

CHAPTER SEVEN
Feelings Follow Actions
79

CHAPTER EIGHT
Prayer is Not About What You Do, But Whose You Are

CHAPTER NINE
Never Let Serving God Get in the Way of Knowing God
93

CHAPTER TEN
Discipline, Desire, Delight
101

CONCLUSION
111

FOREWORD

READING ABOUT A REAL REVIVAL is always inspiring and encouraging. The reader cannot help but wonder what it might be like to be a part of a great move of God and a time of an outpouring of the Holy Spirit. Many of these historical movements took place in towns few have heard of, and involved many whose names might never be well known.

Time will tell, but something like this has been happening with an epicenter at the state university in Huntsville, Texas. For more than twenty years, a great groundswell of young men and women has been stirring and growing, with hearts changed by the power of Christ, and lives called into God's service all across the globe. Hundreds of missionaries have come out of a secular university, taking all that they have learned and experienced, and sharing it. These believers are making disciples who make disciples in campus ministries, churches, and the marketplace around the world.

Alex Rodriguez was one of these young men who came to university with his own ideas about life and the future, only to have everything changed by the great love of Jesus. Alex has been a key part of all that God has done, and all that the Lord has taught the community together. One of our deepest convictions is that we must cultivate our minds to be in love with God—to spend abundant time in the Word of God, praying and talking to the Lord, and thinking deeply about His nature and character. We have to be saturated in truth so that we stand on firm ground as we work together and minister to others.

With his gift of oration and skill with words, Alex captures the best of all we have learned. He has seen and experienced firsthand the fact that this is not just information and encouragement for only one time and one place. We know that your life and ministry can experience radical transformation as you read this book. Walking with God in real devotion impacts a community deeply—from one location to another, and from generation to generation.

Eli and Mary Gautreaux
Chi Alpha Campus Ministries
Huntsville, Texas

INTRODUCTION

R WAS A LITTLE HISPANIC princess with just the right amount of sass to love without losing patience. She was our second foster daughter, our second adventure into a system where non-birth parents attempt to give children a normal life during this abnormal process.

Foster parenting was not our dream, but it became our chosen reality. After five years of trying to build a family, after five years of prayers and unanswered prayers where reality battles theology, we chose to become foster parents. This decision in large part was due to an old preacher named F.W. Boreham. He had left this earth many score years ago, but not before he put his soul into books.

In an essay on suffering, best read with a cup of coffee in one hand and a writing utensil in the other, my wife and I came across this quote:

TURN YOUR SUFFERING INTO SERVICE[1]
This is what God did when He watched His children become rebels. He grabbed a cross to turn rebels back into sons and daughters. This is what we would do with our unanswered prayers. Become fathers

and mothers to the fatherless and motherless.

Stories of our beloved foster children, among many other stories, are throughout this book. Their identities are hidden according to the policies of the foster department.

Life has lessons. All stories have sermons. This is one of them.

R was special. Every child has an imagination that can bring heaven to earth. She was no different. But unlike her three-year-old counterparts, R had a sense of humor. She was funny, yes, but she also understood what was funny. I always believed this was quite advanced for her age. You expect Jerry Seinfeld to know how to make people laugh. You do not expect a toddler to have a discernment for comedy.

This was most evidenced during our Halloween together, when I heard our beloved three-year-old display sarcasm for the first time. We walked streets throughout New Mexico knocking on the doors of stucco homes for candy.

Many houses had your typical decorations: the standard spider webs, a few fake gravestones with a few fake names to create a few fake chuckles. And, of course, the jack-o-lanterns that look angry, like an old man standing in line at the Department of Motor Vehicles all day. As we walked past these decorations towards the chocolate and the taffy, R would stare through the decor. She would then raise her arms and move her fingers like she was casting a spell to say, "Oooh, scary," in an unimpressed, almost taunting manner.

These decorations were designed for children to think something is real. But she recognized immediately she was looking at something blatantly fake. With no terror impeding her steps, we kept moving with ease from house to house as her candy bag was growing full, and my belief of her going to bed without a sugar high was growing empty. She was laughing. She was smiling. She was joking. She was strutting from one house to another—until her raspy laugh was suddenly silenced.

She came across a house with decorations we had not seen that night.

Introduction

The decoration that stalled her in her tracks was a mechanical skeleton towering ten feet tall. A weathered cape surrounded the object. It was beat up, torn up, but given life with every passing wind. It had bones that looked like they were taken straight from a casket. It had eyes large and red with anger, filled with pupils dark as night. One arm was hidden by the cloak. You did not know where it was. You did not know where it was about to be. The other arm was stretched out with a long, ghostly finger pointing directly at all who froze still by its sight.

R, who was filled with life the entire night, was now as idle as death. Her adventurous night of conquering fears was now being conquered by fear. This situation had to be remedied for a victorious night, for a child's imagination, for sweet dreams, for present causes and future effects. I walked up to the decoration, revealing to her the chord that gave this creature power. I explained it was no different than the batteries in her doll or in her piano that play songs with just one touch.

"This is a toy." I grabbed the bones. To my relief and to hers, they squeaked like a toy for dogs. I investigated the cloak until I found a small, little tag explaining this did not come from a cemetery, it came from a country. In every way possible, with numerous sentences and elaboration of paragraphs, I explained to her, "This is not real," because the decoration looked so convincing!

Many of us can tell what is blatantly fake. A plastic grave with a pun for a name? Any child can identify this. An expensive watch with the name of the company misspelled? Any teenager can identify this. An email from a foreign prince asking for help with money they will pay back? Any adult can identify this. We can tell what is blatantly fake. But what is deceitfully lifeless can fool us unless someone identifies what is actually real. This is the purpose of the Parable of the Tares in Matthew 13:24-30, which reads:

> Another parable He put forth to them, saying: "The kingdom of heaven is like a man who sowed good seed in his field; but while

men slept, his enemy came and sowed tares among the wheat and went his way. But when the grain had sprouted and produced a crop, then the tares also appeared. So the servants of the owner came and said to him, "Sir, did you not sow good seed in your field? How then does it have tares? He said to them, "An enemy has done this." The servants said to him, "Do you want us to go up and gather them up?" But he said, "No, lest while you gather up the tares you also uproot the wheat with them. Let both grow together until the harvest, and at the time of harvest I will say to the reapers, "First gather together the tares and bind them in bundles and burn them, but gather the wheat into my barn."

We can tell what is blatantly fake, but what is deceitfully lifeless can fool us until it is too late, especially if we are sleeping when the false seed is sown.

This is a common theme of the Bible. Judas was in small group! He made every meeting. He went out on every mission. He could recite every word Jesus taught.

During the Last Supper, Jesus told all the disciples, "One of you will betray Me" (John 13:21).

The disciples were perplexed at the idea one of them could ever betray their Savior.

Jesus elaborated, "It is he to whom I shall give a piece of bread when I have dipped it" (John 13:26). He then dipped the bread, gives it to Judas, and told him, "What you do, do quickly" (John 13:27).

But none of the other disciples understood why He would tell Judas such a thing!

The disciples had not forgotten what Jesus had said. Their perplexity over someone betraying Jesus was evident. They could not believe Judas, a disciple like the rest of them, would betray the Lord!

Likewise, the devil was a worship leader! He worked in heaven, but he was filled with hell! With his mouth he praised the Lord, but in his

Introduction

heart he said, "I will ascend into heaven, I will exalt my throne above the stars of God; I will also sit on the mount of the congregation on the farthest sides of the north; I will ascend above the heights of the clouds, I will be like the Most High" (Isa. 14:13-14).

Some angels were so impressed with his responsibility and leadership, they sided with the devil, believing it was God who must have done something wrong in a war that split heaven and birthed hell.

How does this happen?

Judas had community with the greatest apostles in history, but missed God! The devil had responsibility of leading angels in song, but missed God! Community was not enough. Responsibility was not enough.

With these present but devotion missing, they became deceitfully lifeless to the point they fooled others—especially themselves!

Is history repeating itself?

I have no ambition to call anyone a devil! But, may I suggest, we are still betraying Jesus with a kiss. We embrace the community that small group ministry provides. We thrive in the responsibility that ministerial leadership and volunteering provides. But devotion is often missing.

Today, many of us go to church with God, but we do not take Him home with us. We "amen" sermons with our mouths, but keep our souls away from altars.

Many of us identify as Christian, but cannot explain why beyond a sinner's prayer. We defend beliefs saying, "It is in the Bible," but we do not know where; we do not know for sure. We have just heard, "It's in the Bible."

Through a lack of understanding the joy of prayer, many of us treat conversing with the living God as an emergency parachute instead of a daily delight. Worship has accidentally been confined to songs and slides. Thought lives have been limited to Sundays. Community is enjoyed. Responsibility is had.

But if devotion is missing, God is missing. If God is missing, community is lacking God's fullness, and responsibility is lacking God's power!

All of this has created a dilemma within Christianity. We are not lacking converts, but we are lacking disciples.

As I write this, church curriculum is the best it has ever been. However, biblical illiteracy is the worst it has ever been with less than thirty-three percent of American churchgoers reading the Bible daily.[2]

Worship services have the excellence of a Broadway play. Yet even the most "faithful" churchgoers have been reduced to three out of every ten Christians.[3]

Conference after conference, book after book, podcast after podcast are produced to help the Christian become a better leader. But this is all futile if the Christian is not becoming a better Christian!

We have tried new strategies and methods to win the lost and deepen the found. We have done this in the attempt to have eternal life as opposed to being deceitfully lifeless. Yet, all the while, Jesus still promises His victorious presence through one disciplined action: "He who abides in Me....bears much fruit.....for without Me you can do nothing" (John 15:5).

Is it possible that what the world needs from the people of God are not better curriculum, or extravagant services, or smarter leaders, but people desperate to be with God?

Is it possible we are so engaged in the familiar "whats" of the gospel—like building small groups, making disciples, serving the needy, and reaching the lost—that we have made the "whys" of the gospel unfamiliar to our souls?

If the examples of Judas and the devil have taught us anything, it is that Christian culture is deceitfully lifeless without Christian conviction. What Christians do will never be real if it is disconnected from revelation and awe of why we do it.

With that being said, this book is written with the conviction of John 15 in mind: We need to make disciples. That is fruit. But we must

Introduction

first be disciples. That is abiding.

We must fulfill the "whats" of the gospel—that is devotion—but not without being fully convicted on the "whys" of the gospel. That is real devotion.

This book is not meant to be an exhaustive end-all, be-all book answering every orthodoxy (correct belief) question and addressing every orthopraxy (correct conduct) issue. It is meant to be a brief introduction to a Christian's understanding of God. It is intended for anyone looking to be a disciple and anyone looking to make disciples.

These chapters contain portable, memorable statements that were discipled into me at the Chi Alpha Campus Ministries of Sam Houston State University in Huntsville, Texas—my first experience in discovering the unfamiliar "whys" behind the familiar "whats" of the gospel. I am grateful to this ministry as it taught me theological truths in laymen's terms. This book attempts to do the same.

Real Devotion is split into two parts: Foundational Principles and Faithful Practices.

In the Foundational Principles of *Real Devotion*, we will look at the unfamiliar "whys" behind familiar beliefs:

Why does God declare salvation is more than doing right things?
Why did God make laws like the Ten Commandments?
Why is God serious about sin?
Why is God Lord? Why cannot I be Lord?
Why does love matter?

In the Faithful Practices of *Real Devotion*, we will look at the unfamiliar "whys" behind familiar behaviors:

Why does humility, or lack thereof, affect our perception of God, self, and others?
Why is self-denial the way for self-fulfillment?

Real Devotion

Why can earthly people pray to a heavenly God?
Why does serving God differ from knowing God?
Why do discipline and delight go together?

Answering these questions will help us discover the transformational power that turns soldiers into sons and daughters, rebels into worshipers, and those who want to quit Jesus into those who have the grit to keep going for God.

Before we come and die for Jesus, we must come and see Him!

This is where real devotion begins! We must see God clearly! We must understand Him rightly!

Let's discover the heart of God again. Let's journey to make the "whys" of the gospel familiar once more.

PART I
Foundational Principles:
Unfamiliar Whys Behind Familiar Beliefs

Real Devotion

CHAPTER ONE

Motive is,
"Why Do You Do the Things You Do, and Who Do You Do Them For?"

MY WIFE, ABBY, AND I, were the Chi Alpha Campus Ministry directors at New Mexico State University for six years. Part of our job was mission trips, arguably the most fun and fearful aspect of college ministry.

This is because, on mission trips, students make a foreign place their home for seven days. They minister to strangers who become friends within a week. They experience real devotion and real community and real responsibility in a short time that can motivate them full time, all of which is the fun part.

The fearful part is that college students, at any given time, can display a mind of their own, or be absent of mind. This can result in many students becoming lost on these trips. There is nothing more fearful then arriving back home with less students than you left with!

Many of these students get lost within airports. This is why one of our trip rules for traveling through an airport is for a leader to be at the front of the group while another leader is at the back of the group. Because without fail, a few students will fall behind. It is never because they walk at a slower pace, but because they are occupied doing numerous, different things as they travel through an airport.

Some students study while they walk. Others have their heads deep into a book. Some are taken up in a conversation. But most of the time, it is a few guys flirting with a few girls. This is not stereotypical. This is a social study. We go on mission trips to serve Jesus, but college students are also hoping for a conversation with the opposite sex they can over-analyze later with their roommates.

College graduates know this was true. College students know this is true!

And when these college students are busy doing everything as they make their way through an airport, they lose sight of the people they are a part of and begin to follow the larger crowd they are around. The people they are a part of head down Terminal B. The crowd they are around head down Terminal A. And without being conscious of it, these busy students falling behind head down the wrong terminal.

It is at this point I have to yell at them to get their attention and bring them back to where they are supposed to be and with whom they are supposed to be with, because they are lost and they do not know they are lost.

They became mistakenly lost because they gave so much attention to what they were doing that they neglected who they were actually with. This happens too often.

Have you ever been mistakenly lost? Have you ever been lost because you were so busy doing something you neglected to be aware of who you were actually with?

This is the essence of something Jesus Himself said:

Not everyone who says to Me, "Lord, Lord," shall enter the kingdom of heaven, but he who does the will of My Father in heaven. Many will say to Me in that day, "Lord, Lord, have we not prophesied in Your name, cast out demons in Your name, and done many wonders in Your name?" And then I will declare to them, "I never knew you; depart from Me, you who practice lawlessness" (Matt. 7:21-23).

Meaning, many are lost, and do not know they are lost because they are too busy doing something that they pay no attention to who they are doing it with!

This is the great theme of the Sermon on the Mount, an entire sermon in which Jesus illuminated subtle contrasts with severe consequences.

There are two types of salt, but the one void of flavor is thrown out (Matt. 5:13).

There are two types of light, but one is placed under a basket (Matt. 5:14-15).

There are two types of giving, but one God does not receive (Matt. 6:1-4).

There are two types of prayer, but one God does not hear (Matt. 6:5-7).

There are two types of fasting, but one God does not see (Matt. 6:16-18).

There are two types of treasure, but one is empty of worth (Matt. 6:19-21).

There are two types of servants, but one despises his master (Matt. 6:24).

There are two types of gates, but one leads to destruction (Matt. 7:13-14).

There are two types of prophets, but one is a wolf in sheep's clothing (Matt. 7:15).

There are two types of trees, but only one bears good fruit (Matt. 7:16-20).

There are two types of houses that experience inevitable storms, but only one thrives through the tribulation (Matt. 7:24-29).

And, of course, the heartbeat of the sermon, our text in Matthew

7:21-23: There are two types of religious people who call Jesus "Lord," prophesy and drive out demons and perform many wonders, but only one who does the will of the Father and enters the kingdom of heaven.

This sermon must have been received with stunning silence as Jesus made it undeniably clear that we can behave completely right and be completely wrong! People prophesied, drove out demons, and performed supernatural wonders, and Jesus said they were unsaved! Meaning, ministry does not equal salvation.

People accurately identified Jesus as Lord, and He still called them unsaved. Meaning, theology does not equal salvation.

People prayed and gave and fasted, and Jesus said He did not know them. Meaning, morality does not equal salvation.

This truth begs the question: Why can people do good things, even ministerial things, and be utterly lost? Charles Spurgeon has an old sermon anecdote that may answer our question.

> Once upon a time there was a king who ruled over everything in a land. One day there was a gardener who grew an enormous carrot.
>
> He took it to his king and said, "My lord, this is the greatest carrot I've ever grown or ever will grow; therefore, I want to present it to you as a token of my love and respect for you."
>
> The king was touched and discerned the man's heart, so as he turned to go, the king said, "Wait! You are clearly a good steward of the earth. I want to give a plot of land to you freely as a gift so you can garden it all."
>
> The gardener was amazed and delighted and went home rejoicing. But there was a nobleman at the king's court who overheard all this, and he said, "My! If that is what you get for a carrot, what if you gave the king something better?"

Chapter One

The next day the nobleman came before the king, and he was leading a handsome black stallion. He bowed low and said, "My lord, I breed horses, and this is the greatest horse I've ever bred or ever will; therefore, I want to present it to you as a token of my love and respect for you."

But the king discerned his heart and said, "Thank you," and took the horse and simply dismissed him. The nobleman was perplexed, so the king said, "Let me explain. That gardener was giving me the carrot, but you were giving yourself the horse."[4]

This is selfishness. Selfishness is consumed with what is best for me at the expense of others. Likewise, to do anything to exalt and satisfy self, even if it is ministry or theology or morality, is selfishness consumed with what is best for me at the expense of God.

Why can people do good things, even ministerial things, and be utterly lost? Although it is possible to have the right method, the Lord is more concerned with the right motive.

A few biblical figures will confirm this as true. As mentioned in the introduction, while leading worship in heaven, the devil became lost as hell. His perfect talent was dismissed because of his wicked heart.

While being in the small group of Jesus for three years, Judas called Him "Teacher," but never called Christ "Lord." He denied Christ before He denied Christ.

Pharisees had all the morality of giving and praying, but Jesus called them a "brood of vipers" and "white washed tombs" (Matt. 12:34; 23:27).

Hosea 6:6 declares that the Lord desires mercy not sacrifice, the knowledge of God more than burnt offerings. It is not enough to do the right things. One can do the right things and be the wrong person. What distinguishes someone as right or wrong, true or false, has nothing to do with methods and everything to do with motive.

How, then, does one know they have clean hands and a pure heart?

How does one know they have chosen the narrow gate, are bearing the good fruit, and living in a house built on the rock?

It is no mistake. Jesus preaches that not everyone will enter the kingdom of heaven, "but he who does the will of My Father in heaven." He declares He will tell many, "I never knew you, depart from Me"—losing enteral life.

Later on, in His prayer in John 17, Jesus defines eternal life: "They would know You, the only true God, and Jesus Christ whom You have sent" (17:3).

Salvation is to know Jesus! The will of God is to know Jesus! This is not merely doing something under God. For many people have brought Him religious service when the Lord really wanted them to know Him.

This is not merely being around God, for Judas was around Jesus, yet not a part of Jesus. The devil was in heaven, yet filled with hell.

Salvation is being for God.

Here is the apostle Paul declaring his own ambition for pulpits: "Him (Christ) we preach" (Col. 1:28, *parenthesis mine*).

Here is Joshua declaring to a nation how his house will be governed: "We will serve the Lord" (Josh. 24:15).

Here is David, in earnest desire of purity, asking God: "Search me, O God, and know my heart, and see if there is any wicked way in me" (Ps. 139:23-24).

The people that please God, the runners that finish the race, the ones who enter through the narrow gate, bear the good fruit and build a house upon solid rock are not the ones with right methods; they are the people with unchanging, right motive. Motive determines our rightness with God.

As an old friend has said, "Motive is, 'Why do you do the things you do, and who do you do them for?'"

Am I in ministry to make disciples for Jesus or to make a name for myself? Am I praying to be heard by God or applauded by men? Am I

Chapter One

learning Him to learn Him or sound like a scholar to the surrounding society? Am I pioneering a ministry for God or for pats on the back from those who watch me leave? Am I giving the Lord or myself the carrot? Am I giving the Lord or myself the horse?

Motive is, "Why do you do the things you do, and who do you do them for?"

May our answer always be that we do what we do for the Jesus who was rich but became poor, so we can be transformed from poverty to riches.

May our service always be for the Jesus who knew no sin but became sin, so we can be transformed from sinners into sons and daughters of God.

Real devotion starts here. If we want to be right with God, He must become the answer to why I do the things I do, and who I do them for.

Real Devotion

CHAPTER TWO

God's Law is Not a Motivation for Obedience, But a Description of Reality from an Infinite Perspective

IN OUR LAST CHAPTER, we learned good theology, active ministry, even obedient morality are nothing without right motive. "Why do we do the things we do, and who do we do them for?" This self-inspection will always reveal whether our heart is filled with purity or perversion.

This question is equally helpful to apply to God: "Why does God do the things He does, and who does He do them for?"

This God-inspection, if attempted with a pure heart, will always find God innocent and brilliant and good. Which leads us to our next chapter: "Why does God define the laws of what is right and what is wrong the way He does?"

We are familiar with God's laws, a few of which we will cover, but why do these laws of God exist?

Growing up, my parents had a very unique way to motivate their children's obedience.

Every child loves presents. This means every child loves Christmas Day because Santa gives them presents. This means every child is looking forward to Christmas Day, no matter if it's December 24th or December 26th. Which, of course, means every child can have tendencies to love Santa Claus more than their actual parents.

After all, children grow up knowing Santa gives them candy on Christmas, but their parents give them carrots for dinner. Children know Santa works in the North Pole surrounded by snow and elves. These same children know their parents work in offices surrounded by suits and briefcases. Children watch movies made about Santa driving a sleigh led by magical reindeer. These same children watch their parents drive them to school in a 2012 Toyota Prius.

Of course children care more about what Santa thinks than what their parents think!

This is why many parents motivate their children's obedience by utilizing the jolly old man who makes lists and checks them twice.

Before there was ever an elf on a shelf, the Rodriguez children were made very aware that if they so much as did or said anything wrong, Santa Claus would be watching them like a hawk from the sky. This was Kris Kringle's snow globe; we were all just living in it!

Our motivation to do our chores was to get a Super Nintendo. Our motivation to not curse was to avoid a stocking of socks which Mom rightfully believed was worse than coal—a statement every child agrees with—and every middle-aged man in need of new socks disagrees with.

With that being said, this is how the commands of our childhood went down: "Do right so Santa will give you presents. Do wrong and Santa will not come to our house!"

This motivates a child! But if the reward is perceived as being not that magnificent, if the punishment is perceived as being not that deplorable, then the motivation for obedience based on punishment or reward loses its power.

This sounds similar to atheists unphased by an eternal heaven or hell: If God is make-believe, then heaven and hell are make-believe. This sounds like lukewarm Christians, who, biblically speaking, are not Christians, disregarding God's commands because they disbelieve a

Chapter Two

God of love would spew them out of His mouth (Rev. 3:16).

If you do not believe in a giver of punishment or reward, if you do not believe in the punishment or the reward, then what weight would any command have in your life? Rules would be merely motivations for obedience. But if you are not motivated, why obey the rule?

In my father's house, losing money or a weekend was a small price to pay for being your own ruler. Receiving money or a gift was a small fee to receive for following the ruler. With these small motivations, we did what we wanted within this economy of punishment and reward.

But this disregard for rules and the rule-giver found its culmination one night when my brother was caught breaking our father's laws, changing the economy of rules and rebellion forever.

The rule at hand was Dad's law to always be home before midnight, a responsibility given with the reason, "Nothing good happens past midnight."

This, however, did not stop my brother's master plan, at the age of fifteen, to sneak out of the house at two in the morning, stealing the keys to Dad's company car in order to drive fifty miles roundtrip to see a girl.

I am not sure how the events of this night unfolded. Perhaps my little brother was too loud stumbling about in the dark. Perhaps the dog outside gave him away. Perhaps Dad's military background made him aware to whatever, whenever, being done by whomever. All I know is my little brother was caught red-handed.

I woke up at three in the morning to the sound of my Dad's yelling voice becoming weak. I jumped out of bed like any sibling desiring to be a spectator of punishment when they are not the culprit. As I walked toward the living room where he had my brother seated, I did not hear Dad scolding him, but reasoning with him.

"Son, nothing good happens past midnight! You do not have your license. The police will punish you for breaking the law. (In Texas that is a $500 ticket for strike one, with a $2,000 ticket for strike two, and up to six months in jail, pending your judge, for strike three). There goes your financial plans."

My father continued, more passionate with every reason he articulated.

"Drunk drivers are all over the city. Thousands have died this year alone. You could get killed and there goes your life! There is only one thing you do with a girl past midnight! You do not have protection; you could wind up with a baby you never planned for from a girl you never planned to be with, and there goes your freedom!"

As he was yelling all of this through loss of breath and cracks in his voice, I noticed my dad, who never cries, was crying.

It became clear in this moment that he was not preaching what is suggestion but what is reality from his forty-five years of experience and perspective that had seen what is true, an experience and perspective which his fifteen-year-old son's understanding failed in comparison.

"Do not drive without a license" understands the science of law enforcement.

"Do not get hit by a drunk driver" understands the science of collision.

"Do not sleep with people" understands the science of sex (and assumes the responsibility of fatherhood).

It became clear in this moment that my father's law had evolved. Or perhaps we matured. Either way, our view of his commands was now entirely different.

After that, we did not merely believe in the punishment of rebellion. We did not merely believe in the reward of obedience. We believed in the reason for the rules. My dad's laws were not motivations for obedience, but descriptions of reality based on what is true from a life that has seen more.

This foundation is true of all man-made laws.

"Do not speed" reflects the results of people driving however they want.

Chapter Two

"No guns allowed" was written because of what happens when people bring weapons into schools.

"No fake ID's" is on the books because of what happens when immature people pretend to be mature people, and wrong people cascade as the right people.

These are good laws originating from people with finite perspectives!

How much more weight, then, must be given to an infinite perspective? Mankind has made rules from the start of civilization. But there is a God who has existed before civilization and who will outlast all civilizations!

Humanity has learned what is true from a limited beginning to direct them to a better end. God is the Beginning and the End!

Therefore, when it comes to God's laws, Winkie Pratney rightly articulates them this way: "God's laws are not motivations for obedience, but descriptions of reality from an infinite perspective."[5] They are not based on what could happen, but on reality that does happen, for opinions by nature cannot exist within an omniscient nature.

Do you see, then, the audacity of someone hearing God's descriptions of reality and ignoring them?

If a person tells us he wants to go to the top of a one hundred story building and jump off, assuring us he will fly perfectly to the bottom and land on both feet, completely convinced gravity is a suggestion or theory but not possibly reality, we will call him crazy!

In the history of the world, no man has attempted to fly off a one hundred story building and lived to tell about it! To disregard reality is to disregard sanity.

This is precisely the judgment for anyone who hears God's descriptions of reality and willingly ignores them.

Consider a few of God's commands for application:

Ezekiel 18:20 gives us a most haunting verse, "The soul who sins shall die."

This is not motivation for obedience. This is not a suggestion of what could be. This is the Lord saying He has seen all possible outcomes of all possible sins from all possible times, and every time the ending is the same, "The soul who sins shall die." Selfishness always leads to a grave. To disregard this law of God and sin anyway is to disregard sanity.

Likewise, when a person reads Matthew 28:19-20—"Go therefore and make disciples of all the nations, baptizing them in the name of the Father and of the Son and of the Holy Spirit, teaching them to observe all things that I have commanded you; and lo, I am with you always, even to the end of the age"—this is not motivation for obedience. This is not suggestion of what could be. This is the Lord saying His manifest presence is evoked by His people's missional responsibility.

He is the Bridegroom rushing to His Bride's side as we try to produce spiritual children. He is the Father rushing to His children's side as we fight for our brothers and sisters. He is the King by His soldiers' side as we attempt to claim new land for the kingdom. He is the Savior by His helpers' side as we attempt to rescue people from peril.

The promise of His presence is contingent on the practice of discipleship. To not do the practice of discipleship is to lose the promise of His presence.

To believe we can be stagnant for Jesus but still have the presence of Jesus is insane! Why would God change conditional promises for a rebel's conveniences? To disregard this law of God by not making disciples is to disregard sanity.

Let us look at a few more laws to ensure we understand this truth.

When the Lord speaks through the apostle Paul in Colossians 3:13, "Forgive one another (NIV)," He knows forgiveness offers freedom to the one forgiven and the one forgiving!

This is from the Lord who forgave all humanity through the death of His Son on a cross. He knows forgiveness leads to a resurrected life for the forgiving, but a dead grave for the ones who refuse to forgive.

Do you see God's description of reality from an infinite perspective? He is commanding forgiveness, knowing bitterness is the poison we

Chapter Two

drink as we wait for someone else to die.

When the Lord says in Matthew 5:28 to not look lustfully, this is the God of infinite perspective understanding that loving one another makes us more complete people (John 17:21), but lusting turns a person into a body, and a person in need of completion into a monster hell-bent on self-gratification.

Do you see God's description of reality from an infinite perspective?

Lust desensitizes the dignity of sex, making it no longer personal, but merely physical. This desensitizes the dignity of people as we treat one another less like an individual and more like an object.

When the Lord speaks through the apostle in 1 Thessalonians 5:17, "Pray without ceasing," this is the God of infinite perspective understanding that prayer brings a perfect heaven down to an imperfect earth. Prayer grows one's communication with God, which always grows one's communion with God, which always grows one's likeness to God.

Do you see God's description of reality from an infinite perspective?

To pray without ceasing is to have more heaven and less earth, both around you and within you. To disregard the law of God, no matter the command in question, is to experience Ezekiel 18:20, "The soul who sins shall die."

But to live according to these laws and align with reality is to experience Psalm 1:1-3:

> Blessed is the one who does not walk in step with the wicked or stand in the way that sinners take or sit in the company of mockers, but whose delight is in the law of the Lord, and who meditates on His law day and night. That person is like a tree planted by streams of water, which yields its fruit in season and whose leaf does not wither—whatever they do prospers (NIV).

God's laws are not motivations for obedience; they are descriptions of reality from an infinite perspective. To ignore God's reality is to die.

Real Devotion

But to abide by His reality is to prosper in whatever we do.

CHAPTER THREE

Sin is Not the Breaking of Impersonal Law, But the Personal Heart of God

WE HAVE JUST DISCOVERED that the laws of God are not motivations to receive a reward like heaven or avoid a punishment like hell. They are descriptions of reality from God's infinite perspective. His laws are not opinions; they are the result of His goodness and all-knowing nature telling us what is real.

This explains the commands of God. To obey them is to prosper in whatever you do, as the Psalmist said, and to disobey them is to die, as the prophet Ezekiel has said.

Although the prophet makes clear what happens to the sinner because of sin, what happens to God because of sin? The answer to this question will tell us what sin really is.

My wife and I were foster parents for three years. Like any relationship, it was a roller coaster with ups and downs. But we loved it.

In our third year, we brought two twin eight-year-old boys into our home. They were sweet boys who loved what boys love. They knew every dinosaur by name and fact, habitually expressing dominance over me in dinosaur trivia. They played cops and robbers with Nerf guns, and could be overheard exclaiming in their best deep voice impersonation, "Don't make do this!"

They watched superheroes and dressed up as superheroes, and no matter what the comic books said about their characters, every hero they pretended to be could fly.

Can you imagine a Gotham City protected by a Batman who can actually fly like Superman? There would be no crime, and perhaps no taxes.

Watching these twin brothers love what boys love was easy. Watching these twin brothers try to love one another was a problem.

All foster children are coming from trauma. They are victims of someone else's selfishness. Is this not the case with selfishness?

A quick study of Achan and Ai will reveal individual selfishness always has community consequences. Selfishness effects more than the person committing it.

Our boys were affected by looking at familiar people and believing they did not know them anymore. Being disconnected from their own house resulted in their own relationship with each other becoming disconnected.

They did not know how to live with one another anymore, evidenced by fights over everything. There was dismay over small things and big things. No trespass was considered minimal. Yes, tension is inevitable between siblings as they grow up. Their trauma, however, amplified this tension as these boys forgot how to love one another.

It became clear to my wife and me that we had to help these brothers relearn how to be friends. To accomplish this, we began to articulate rules that would build their relationship.

Before, during, and after a fight would break out, the boys would hear, "Do to others what you would have them do to you" (Matt. 7:12, NIV).

"Do you want someone to shoot a Nerf gun directly at your face?" "Do you want someone to tell a girl you like them if you do not like

Chapter Three

them?" "Do you want someone to tell a girl you like them if you do like them?" "Do you want someone pretending to be a giant monster and kicking down your Lego buildings?" "Do you want someone eating all of your candy?" "Do you want someone stealing all of your candy?" "Do you want someone stealing all of your candy without you knowing it and then selling it back to you at a steep price?"

As fights over trivial things would persist at school and home, we began to drop them off at school, telling them: "Boys, we love you. Please remember, you cannot fight every fight."

More descriptions of reality continued: "Do I need to complain about my brother playing with my friends at recess?"

"Is having pepperoni pizza worse than having no pizza for dinner?"

"Can't both of you have the same pretend superpowers? Have not multiple comic book universes co-existed by doing just that?"

"Is it really a spoiler alert if you have both seen *Jurassic World* twenty times and you both know who is about to die?"

Slowly, but surely, the boys began to relearn how to be friends with one another. By no means was offense eliminated, but there was less of it.

"Do unto others as you would have them do unto you." "You cannot fight every fight." "Think before you speak." "If you obey more, you get more; if you obey less you get less."

That was the purpose of these commands: To help them become friends again.

In the same manner, the commands of God were given to help people relearn how to be friends with Him.

Israel had lived in slavery surrounded by the sinfulness of Egypt. God's name was becoming unfamiliar as Egyptian gods became familiar. God's laws were ignored as Egyptian customs became common. Discovering God's friendship was replaced with discovering one's self—a practice as old as time and destructive as death.

When the Lord delivered His people from slavery in the land of

Egypt, they still had the culture of Egypt poisoning their hearts (Acts 7:39). They had left the land, but the land had not left them. A change of place did not equal a change of character.

This is why the Ten Commandments were given. Laws were needed to help rebels learn how to be friends with God again.

To paraphrase a sermon by Eli Stewart:

If someone does not know how to be friends with you, you have to teach them by instructing them in the most obvious of things they simply do not know.

"If we are going to be friends, when you come over to my house do not try to seduce my wife. Friends do not take each other's spouses."

"If we are going to be friends, when you come over to my house, you cannot take whatever is in my wallet. Friends do not steal each other's money."

"If we are going to be friends, when you come over to my house, you cannot talk about something meaningless all day, every day, as if it is life itself. Friends do not waste each other's worth."[6]

Eli Stewart concludes, "What are these but reflections of the commandments? Do not take my spouse is, 'You shall not commit adultery' (Ex. 20:14). Do not take my money is, 'You shall not steal' (Ex. 20:15). Do not waste my worth is, "You shall have no other gods before Me" (Ex. 20:3).

God's laws are descriptions of reality from an infinite perspective. This is their nature. Obedience to these laws help people become friends with God. This is their purpose.

God's rules do not just define reality, they develop relationship, telling us what to do and what not do to be friends with God.

Chapter Three

Laws, then, are not impersonal. Obedience to laws is actually meant to progress the personal between man and God. If God's laws are personal, then what would be the destruction of breaking His law?

In Genesis 6:5-6, we have one of the most profound verses describing sin and its effect.

> Then the LORD saw that the wickedness of man was great in the earth, and that every intent of the thoughts of his heart was only evil continually. And the LORD was sorry that He had made man on the earth, and He was grieved in His heart.

The word "sorry" is the same Hebrew word for "repent." The familiar definition of repent is, "To change one's mind." Although repentance means no less than this, the Hebrew word has another meaning: "to lose one's breath."

Genesis 6 is telling us God saw the wickedness of humanity was great in the earth, exemplified by every thought of man's heart being consistently evil, and this depravity caused the Lord to lose His breath.

Have you ever lost your breath? This is an attribute associated with the panic of heartbreak. Watching a life vanish before one's eyes has this effect. Seeing a loved one at a funeral in clothes they did not choose has this effect. Every time death is involved, the panic of heartbreak can cause one to lose their breath.

This is the picture of Genesis 6: The Lord who loved humanity lost His breath as we, through our own choices for vices, became less than human!

Walks in the cool of the evening with God had been replaced with running from God. Trusting God had been replaced with doubting God. Bowing to God had been replaced with trying to be God.

Every imagination of the thoughts of our hearts was only evil continually as we consumed ourselves with wickedness!

God watched His beloved people die by choosing depravity in

complete antithesis to the thoughts and dreams He had for them, and it caused God to lose His breath with the panic of heartbreak.

I hope the principle of this scripture is clear. God is personally effected by sin. This effect within God found its culmination with the death of Jesus on a cross. But, as George Otis, Jr., suggests, although Jesus died on a cross, He did not die from a cross.

In biblical times, it took close to a week for crucifixion to kill the body through blood loss and bodily malfunction. Criminals would hang and die a slow death within a matter of days.

Yet Jesus died a quick death within a matter of hours. Reflecting on tendencies, if ninety-nine out of a hundred people experience the same fate in the same time but one person ruins the curve, is there something now different about the system? Or is there something different about the individual?

We must remember the divinity of Jesus means that although He is human with a finite body, He is also God with an infinite spirit. There is no one like Him.

Within this finite heart of Jesus is an infinite love for all people. As John tells us, "For God so loved the world that He gave His only begotten Son" (John 3:16). As Hebrews 12:2 tells us, "For the joy that was set before Him endured the cross."

Furthermore, within this finite mind of Jesus is infinite thoughts for people. As Jeremiah declared, "For I know the thoughts that I think toward you, says the Lord" (Jer. 29:11, NKJV). This is a significant amount of intimacy. To be precise, it is an infinite amount of intimacy. Intimacy with any degree always comes with the cost of grief.

C.S. Lewis has said:

There is no safe investment. To love at all is to be vulnerable. Love anything, and your heart will certainly be wrung and possibly be broken. If you want to make sure of keeping it intact, you must give your heart to no one, not even to an animal. Wrap it carefully round

Chapter Three

with hobbies and little luxuries; avoid all entanglements; lock it up safe in the casket or coffin of your selfishness.

But in that casket—safe, dark, motionless, airless—it will change. It will not be broken; it will become unbreakable, impenetrable, irredeemable. The alternative to tragedy, or at least to the risk of tragedy, is damnation.

The only place outside heaven where you can be perfectly safe from all the dangers and perturbations of love is hell.[7]

To love anyone is to pay the cost of grief. The boy next door will have a broken heart when the beautiful girl next door moves away forever. The teenage girl will be crushed if her boyfriend decides leaving high school means leaving her. The adult spouse will be broken if a marriage ends in divorce or death. Intimacy always comes with the risk of grief, and grief is proportional to intimacy. This is why losing a longtime friend hurts more than losing a short-time acquaintance, but nothing compares to losing a friend of a lifetime.

This must mean the God of infinite intimacy with His beloved people felt infinite grief because of our rebellion. What would be the result of this?

George Otis, Jr., concludes:

Jesus "did not die from from crucifixion, but rather from the internal agony of His soul. Crucifixion merely facilitated His death. No man took the life of Jesus. He died as a result of a voluntary identification, the sin of the world crushing out His life.[8]

With these serious effects we must be absolutely sure we have no confusion what sin is, lest we die and grieve the heart of God again.

What, then, is sin?

We like to think sin is a few explicit things that everyone would call wrong. In the secular world, we call sin the triggermen of mass shootings, child abusers, and sex traffickers.

In the sacred world, we add to sin's rap sheet fornication, drunkenness, and adultery.

But sin is much larger than this. Sin is not merely a few actions. Sin is the attitude of selfishness, whether it manifests in seemingly wrong actions or seemingly right actions.

"Love....does not seek its own" (1 Cor. 13:5).

"Let nothing be done through selfish ambition" (Phil. 2:3).

"If anyone desires to come after Me, let him deny himself" (Luke 9:23).

"For where envy and self-seeking exist, confusion and every evil thing are there" (James 3:16).

Jesus died on a cross. But He died from the grief of an infinite heart beholding an unlimited amount of people's selfishness—from the pride that calls itself right in its own eyes (Judg. 21:25), to His people's habitual desire to forsake the spring of living water and build up cisterns that cannot hold water (Jer. 2:13), to worshiping worthless idols that made us worthless (2 Kings 17:15).

Our sinfulness broke God's heart and killed Him.

God's personal heart manifests itself as our friend. This means sin is backstabbing.

God's personal heart manifests itself as our Bridegroom. This means sin is cheating.

God's personal heart manifests itself as our king. This means sin is rebellion.

Simply put, sin is not the breaking of an impersonal law, but the breaking of the personal heart of God.

But there is hope. If God's commands are rules for relationship, then to obey God is to become friends with the King of the universe once more.

Chapter Three

Will we repent and believe God is personal? Will we repent and behave as God's friends?

Real Devotion

CHAPTER FOUR

GOD HAS A RIGHT TO OUR LIVES, NOT BECAUSE OF WHAT HE DOES, BUT WHO HE IS

WE HAVE SPENT THE LAST two chapters looking at God's law and the sin that breaks God's heart. I trust you have a greater understanding behind the commands of God and the consequences of sin, both on us and on God.

It is still possible, however, that we are smarter but not holier. After all, some of God's commands are very uncomfortable! Some of our sin is very enjoyable, though it costs everything and is worth nothing!

This is our dilemma: We want to love God, but we also want to be god, too! Cannot God have some of our life while we retain other parts of our life? This question is an issue of commitment, surrender, and whether we carry a cross for the Christ who carried one for us.

Simply put, why does Jesus have to be Lord, not just Savior?

This question must be addressed now, as it is evident people throughout history have attempted to have God as Savior while attempting to be their own lord!

One biblical study of ministry has suggested that only one-out-of-three Christian leaders finished well.[9] We have our King Sauls who lost kingdoms. We have our King Nebuchadnezzars who lost their minds. And, we have our Stephens who lost their lives before the Jesus they saw standing beside the throne.

One-out-of-three leaders finished well! Have we seen the "found" become lost? Have we watched "calling" be replaced by convenience? Have we confessed God, but attempted to be our own god?

Or, have we, like faithful soldiers, endured to the end?

When it comes to the issue of commitment, there are two entirely different reasons a person gives commitment to God. One reason has caused the death of commitment. The other has caused the death of self and life in Christ. Look with me for a moment at why commitment dies.

The Chi Alpha campus ministry at Sam Houston State University has been around for about thirty years. Theirs is a legacy filled with numerous students who have stories to tell. Here is one of them recalled by campus pastors Eli and Mary Gautreaux while speaking at a campus missionary conference in 2018:

> There was a student leader at Sam Houston who had a significant amount of debt. Debt is a burden we are always looking to bury. Like many other college students, she worked her way through college. But her job as a waiter could only cover the bills. It could not conquer her tuition.
>
> Her manager knew her predicament and he had one of his own, so he offered her this ultimatum: "I know you have a lot of debt. I have a lot of money. I also have a nephew who wants to come to America. If you marry my nephew, I will erase all of your debt. I will put you two up in a two-bedroom apartment. You can have your own room that I pay for so there is no cost and no funny business. If your relationship turns into a Will and Grace storyline, we will call that a bonus. All you have to do is stay married for two years. Then, you can leave the marriage with no debt. And he can leave the

Chapter Four

marriage with his green card. Everybody wins."

Does this sound like commitment? Does this sound like love? This is a green card marriage not based on who the person is, but on what they can do for you. The worth is not in the character of a person, but in a circumstantial deal at the expense of a person. There is love for self, but not love for one another. There is devotion, but it has a number of conditions. There is a service, but no satisfaction.

This commitment will die as soon as someone stops doing what we want him or her to do, or if there is no longer a need to do it.

When we hear of such an arrangement, our hearts become broken and our spirits stirred. This is not commitment. This is not love. This is someone being used.

Now, with these same broken hearts and stirred spirits we must ask, "Do we use God?" Is it possible our commitment to Jesus is nothing more than a "green card marriage"? In a green card religion, Jesus is a ticket to heaven, but not heaven Himself. We do not want to bow to Him as king. We do not want to love Him as Bridegroom. We do not want to be with Him as friend. We just want Jesus to be Savior. Nothing less, but also nothing more.

We want Jesus to come down like Superman and save us from peril. But we do not want Clark Kent to stay over for dinner.

For many of us, Jesus is nothing more than a golden ticket to a golden place.

We have heard of a place called heaven, which is described as Paradise, where Jesus dwells. We have also heard of a place called hell where our skin can be singed, where the devil dwells.

Because we prefer a better place over a burdensome one, we bow our heads and close our eyes and raise our hands at the preacher's cue. We ask Jesus to come into our hearts, only to never talk to Him again. We call this "salvation," while making no attempt to discover if God

Himself calls this salvation.

Perhaps we are only interested in the gifts God brings. Like Simon the Sorcerer, we want His power, but do not care for His presence. So we ask for heaven's gifts until we find them beneath our trees, and then we go on with no concern for the Giver.

Perhaps we are only interested in the community that follows. Like Ananias and Sapphira, we believe this Christian community that has found us can never be lost like our souls. So we give God part and tell the community it was all, with no fear or sobriety that we are dead men walking.

Perhaps we are only interested in the reputation that follows. We use God's name to build our own. Ministry and service are used to become known, all the while the only name worth knowing goes unknown.

Committing ourselves to God to get something other than God is unreal devotion. This commitment always dies when God stops doing what we want Him to do, or if there is no longer a need for Him to do it—proving we were never really committed to God. We were committed to ourselves.

If our "why Jesus?" is to not burn in hell, or is to make it to a place called heaven, or is to use God to get anything other than God, then we have not really discovered Jesus, and our Christianity is nothing that will last.

Why, then, must Jesus be the Lord of one's life? Why Christianity?

There is a parable of Jesus found in Matthew 13:44: "The kingdom of heaven is like treasure hidden in a field, which a man found and hid; and for joy over it he goes and he sells all that he has and buys that field."

To borrow the imagination of Mr. Winkie Pratney, this parable can be explained in modern day language like this:

> There is a college student running late to his university class, so he decides to take a shortcut through a field that is for sale. As he is running through this field, he trips over a small pointy box sticking

Chapter Four

out of the ground. After he gets up and looks around to make sure no female saw his failure, he goes closer to this box sticking out of the ground to kick it in anger. Because he is a guy. And we guys believe kicking equals justification—the one belief that has lasted since toddler years.

As he approaches the box, the peculiarity of its age evokes his curiosity. He bends down and proceeds to dig around, for it is clear there is more to this mystery than meets the eye. As his hands are digging underneath the dirt, he notices an opening in the box. He puts his hand in the opening and begins to feel these rock-shaped figures. He pulls one out, dusts it off. His eyes become wide as he realizes this is no ordinary rock. It is a diamond the size of a stone.

He looks around to see if anyone is watching, and then covers up this box so no one can find it. He decides to grab an Uber, although he owns a car, because he wants to be trendy. He then heads to the nearest jewelry store. He greets the store clerk and drops this diamond on the table.

"How much is this worth?" he asks.

The jeweler takes the diamond into his hands for a closer look and tries to hide his excitement. "It's worth fifteen hundred dollars," says the jeweler, completely sweaty, with little to no eye contact.

"Oh," says the college student. "Very well." He exchanges the diamond for money and heads on his way.

If that one diamond was worth fifteen hundred dollars, how many diamonds are in that treasure box? The college student immediately rushes back to the field for sale to find out. He finds the box, ensures no one else is looking, and digs his hands into the dirt to pull out the biggest rock he could get ahold of—a rock the size of a softball.

He covers up the treasure box, grabs another ride to the jeweler, and then drops this softball-sized treasure on the table.

"How about this?" says the college student. "What is this worth?"

The jeweler's jaw drops. With hands shaking he grabs the treasure before his eyes, his eyes widening with closer inspection.

"Where did you get this?" asks the jeweler.

The college student plays it cool, "I just stumbled upon it." A play on words every writer of every Nineties action movie would be proud of. "So how much is it worth?"

The jeweler, without breaking eye contact with the treasure, responds, "I don't know."

The college student inquires, "What do you mean you don't know? You are a jeweler. It is your job to know."

The jeweler then looks the young man in the eye and says, "This is the largest ruby I have ever seen. I cannot begin to tell you what it's worth. It's absolutely priceless, more valuable than you and I could even imagine."

The college student thinks to himself, "This is just one softball-sized ruby, one treasure among countless others inside that box." He then looks for the first opportunity to leave. He runs out of the store. He does not head to the field where he found the treasure,

Chapter Four

but to his apartment. He grabs his Xbox, all his games, takes all the clothes out of his closet, takes the seventy-inch TV off his wall, takes pictures of all his furniture and everything he owns to place on Facebook with prices.

His roommate is freaking out watching all of this. "What are you doing?" he inquires.

The college student responds, "I am going to sell all I have to buy that empty field on the way to school."

The roommate, of course, thinks this young man is crazy. But the college student who found the treasure in the field knows this is the most rational thing to do. To do anything less would actually be crazy and irresponsible. He found something of infinite value making everything else worthless.

So he sold what he could keep to gain a treasure he must not lose.

Winkie Pratney summarizes this principle in the life of the fictional college student and within our very real lives by reminding us of the truth of intrinsic value. "Intrinsic" means something that has value in and of itself, not borrowed worth from something more worthy, but inherent worth.

When we come across intrinsic value, it obligates us to choose it over everything else that is less.

When we come across something of rarity, it has more value, obligating us to choose it over what is all too common. This is why the Toyota Corolla with models made every sixty seconds is less valuable then the Lamborghini Reventon with only thirteen models in the world.

When we come across something of beauty, it has more value, obligating us to choose it over what is all too ordinary. This is why

Hawaii was voted the most popular vacation destination of 2018, not Deming, New Mexico.

When we come across something of purity, it is has more value, obligating us to choose it over what is all too tainted. This is why one carat of cubic zirconia sells for about twenty dollars, and a one-carat diamond sells for about fifteen hundred dollars.

When we come across something of power, it has more value, obligating us to choose it over what is all too lacking.

Rarity, beauty, purity, and power—the Lord does not do these things. The Lord does not go to a separate source to have these things. The Lord is in and of Himself all these things. Jesus is the treasure in the field. He is intrinsically rare. As E. Stanley Jones has said, "Every other religion suggests how evil came into the world. Christianity is the only religion where God says He came to take evil out."[10] He is intrinsically beautiful. This is the God who is a friend of sinners, the God who came to heal the sick, the God who calls not those who think they are righteous, but those who know they are rebels. He is intrinsically pure. His presence makes prophets repent and angels sing, "Holy, Holy, Holy is the Lord of hosts." His presence makes any ground sacred. He is intrinsically powerful. "And He is before all things, and in Him all things consist" (Col. 1:17).

People must go against established paths to become rare. People are beautiful, but beauty fades with age. Purity hinges on laws impossible to obey. Power depends on money that fluctuates and positions that transition from one person to the next. Everything else in this world has to go to something else to become valuable, but Jesus is in and of Himself intrinsically valuable.

His intrinsic value obligates the obedience of our lives.

As Winkie Pratney has so eloquently said, "God has a right to our lives not because of what He does but who He is."[11]

When we surrender to the right Jesus has to our lives not because of what He does but who He is, nothing can move a person away from

Chapter Four

God. We take heart in trouble because Jesus has overcome the world. We throw what crowns we have before the throne of Jesus who is worthy of all glory and honor and power. We believe the Good Shepherd when He says He will be with us during valleys of shadows of death. We finish races because all temporary prizes are nothing compared to being with Jesus, the ultimate prize.

This is why Jesus is Lord. He is intrinsically valuable.

Perhaps commitment evidenced by complete surrender to His lordship is still scary. If a man asks a woman within minutes of meeting her for a devotion through richer or poorer, in sickness and health, until death do they part, that is terrifying! But if the man and woman get to know each other through time and proximity, they will begin to like each other when they discover likable attributes. Through more knowledge of each other, like will turn into love. This love will find its culmination as they confess before family and friends a commitment to each other through being rich or poor, in sickness and in health, 'til death do they part.

This commitment is not scary at all when you know someone is worth it. Therefore, letting God be God of our lives is only scary to the degree we do not know Him. If we will take time to be with God, to have extravagant time with Jesus, surrendering to the lordship of Jesus will not be a scary negotiation, but a sensible surrender.

Real Devotion

CHAPTER FIVE

LOVE FINDS A NEED AND MEETS IT

WE HAVE REACHED THE CONCLUSION of the first part of this book.

By now, we have an understanding of the foundational principles of Christianity informing us on a few unfamiliar "whys" behind the familiar beliefs of the gospel. In the next part of this book, we will look at the faithful practices of Christianity to discover a few unfamiliar "whys" behind the familiar behaviors of one changed by the gospel.

This brings us to the current chapter. It is the bridge. What we are about to get into is both a belief at the heart of the gospel and the key behavior influencing those changed by the gospel. We are going to look at one of the most popular, most defined, and most misinterpreted attributes that exists in the world.

This word has been used to describe affection for a friend. This word has also been used to describe affection for food. This theme appears in the most unromantic adventure movies. This theme finds its influence in almost every song. The entertainment industry has produced multiple definitions of love, many of which are conflicting, catchy, and misleading.

Love is a household word. It is commonly used, but not commonly understood. This is not a new occurrence. The Greeks had four different words for love in an attempt to be unmistakably clear. To be unmistakably comprehensive, Jesus preached the greatest commandment is to, "Love the Lord your God with all your heart, with all your soul, and with all your mind. This is the first and great commandment. And the second is like it: 'You shall love your neighbor as yourself'" (Matt. 22:39).

To be unmistakably coherent, the apostle Paul explains the "nonnegotiable" of this attribute:

> Though I speak with the tongues of men and of angels, but have not love, I have become a sounding brass or a clanging cymbal. And though I have the gift of prophecy, and understand all mysteries and all knowledge, and though I have all faith, so that I could remove mountains, but have not love, I am nothing. And though I bestow all my goods to feed the poor, and though I give my body to be burned, but have not love, it profits me nothing" (1 Cor. 13:1-3).

This is a bold proclamation by the apostle! He is saying that without love, no message and no miracle and no martyrdom is meaningful.

What, then, is love? The apostle elaborates on the content of love:

> Love suffers long (the endurance of love) and is kind (the activity of love); love does not envy (the focus of love); love does not parade itself, is not puffed up (the humility of love); does not behave rudely (the courtesy of love), does not seek its own (the unselfishness of love), is not provoked (the temperament of love), thinks no evil (the thought of love); does not rejoice in iniquity, but rejoices in the truth (the sincerity of love); bears all things, believes all things, hopes all things, endures all things. Love never fails (the longevity of love) (1 Cor. 13:4-7, *words in parenthesis mine*).

Chapter Five

Jesus simplifies this content of love into one action. "Greater love has no one than this, than to lay down one's life for his friends" (John 15:13). After such exposition, there is no doubt our minds are smarter.

But as we have alluded to previously, the goal of Bible study is not merely for smarter minds, but holier souls. How then do we move this love from paper to practicality? How can we take this content of love, and action of love, to define love in the simplest of ways for the most consistent obedience?

Simply put, how and why should we lay down our life for a friend?

I have a good friend named Eric from a small Texas town who has a big Texas attitude. He stands about six-foot-two. He carries broad, former-college-baseball-player shoulders. His cadence hints of his Southern origins. His friendliness knows no stranger. He tends to let unplanned, casual conversations with unknown people delay his plans with the people he actually knows.

I dare say his friendliness is known worldwide, since I found myself sharing a story about Eric in a coffee shop in Almaty, Kazakhstan. This coffee shop was 7,300 miles from the Texas Eric and I identify as home. Yet, somehow, in this Russian-speaking country known more for its oil then its tourists, a fellow American I did not know was "dropping ease" on my story and inquires.

"That Eric from Texas wouldn't be Eric Mingle would it?"

I do not know the odds. But on the other side of the world, I found a man who knows the friendliness of my friend. This makes the story of Eric I am about to share all the more unique.

Many years ago during our time in college, Eric had an old high school friend come into town. It had been a few years since they had seen each other, but it seemed his friend's method of operation had not changed—he was on a hunt for alcohol.

The friend asked if Eric wanted to meet up for old-time's sake. Eric, known across the world for his friendliness, agreed. They rendezvoused at one of the town bars infamously known for trouble. In the belief good company equals brave decisions, Eric asked one of the small group guys he was discipling to come with him.

When they arrived, Eric's friend came to meet him in the parking lot.

Even at thirty feet away, Eric could smell the bar coming off of his friend's breath. Jack Daniels and Johnny Walker have a way of making their presence known. He could see his friend could not walk straight. His speech was slurred.

Eric had to catch him as his friend stumbled into a handshake. It was unmistakably clear to Eric that his old friend was significantly drunk. Eric then insisted his friend stay the night because a three-hour drive home at midnight under those intoxicated circumstances would not be good for him, nor for the hopes and dreams of anyone else on the road.

But his friend, void of all rationality and lacking any sobriety, became furious at the thought of someone else telling him what to do. Eric argued with his friend for fifteen minutes to stay the night and sleep in his house. He would have free lodging. He could sleep in his bed. He would cover gas tomorrow—if only his intoxicated friend would not drive home tonight.

But every argument and suggestion was met by his friend's irrationality and curses.

It became clear to Eric that he only had two options: one, he could let his drunken friend attempt a three-hour drive home at midnight, knowing the risks were high he would never make it; or two, he could stop his friend from flirting with death by any means necessary.

It then dawned on Eric there was only one thing to do. So his six-foot-two frame wound up, and this former college baseball player, who once threw ninety-mile-an-hour fastballs, threw a ninety-mile-an-hour right hook that connected with his friend's jaw. Immediately, the drunk friend dropped to the ground unconscious.

Meanwhile, Eric's small group guy is in the truck watching all this! When Eric punched his friend, this small group guy started freaking

Chapter Five

out!

"I can't believe you knocked him out! I thought you Chi Alpha guys were Christian! Why did you do that?"

Without skipping a beat, Eric looked his disciple straight in the eye and said, "Because over my dead body is he going to live a stupid life."

For the rest of that disciple's life, he never sinned again! He is probably in the third heaven as I write!

The two then proceeded to load Eric's unconscious friend into a vehicle, making it look like the Mafia had come to Huntsville, Texas.

They drove to IHOP and unloaded the unconscious friend into a booth. Eric gave the keys to his small group guy and told him to split because when his friend would inevitably wake up, he was not going to be happy and he did not need to be anywhere near those keys.

Eventually the friend regained consciousness. He then created a massive scene, which was not uncommon to IHOP. After much cursing and yelling, he told Eric his final words, "Eric, I will never forgive you for this! And when I get my truck back and drive home, you and I are done!"

Eric owned up to his actions, saying, "I would rather have you alive and be your enemy, then have you dead because I was a friend who did nothing."

Do friendly people knock out their friends to prevent their death and sustain their life?

Love means standing in the gap between sobriety and stupidity. Love means fighting to move someone from who they are to who they are meant to be, as someone's future-tense potential is always a present-tense responsibility.

Love, according to Jesus, is laying down one's life for a friend. Eric laid down his reputation for a friend. This is uncomfortable.

I could tell you the story of a newlywed named Rob Akin, a country boy who can survive, complete with blatant love for Jesus and hidden sass for mankind—quite the charismatic combination.

A few months into marriage, his lovely bride discovered she needed a new kidney, and quickly. Time was on the line. Health was on the line. The ministry they were apart of announced the need for prayer.

What ensued was more than prayer.

"I will give her one of my kidneys," said a friend of the bride.

"I will give her one of mine," said a complete stranger to the bride.

"She can take mine," said a young man who could not have been more than eighteen years of age.

"She can have mine," said a young lady who was not but a month into the ministry.

This rally proves the wise words of Mother Theresa:

> I used to pray that God would feed the hungry or do this or that, but now I pray that He will guide me to do whatever I'm supposed to do, what I can do. I used to pray for answers, but now I'm praying for strength. I used to believe that prayer changes things, but now I know that prayer changes us and we change things.[12]

Prayer changed the hearts of these people. They were not simply going to ask for something; they were going to do something. But one voice was heard above the rest as Rob himself stepped forward, in the spirit of sickness and in health, through prosperity and adversity. He declared, "She will have my kidney."

Rob laid down his body for his wife. This is sacrificial.

I could tell you the story of Emmet Rumfield, a skater boy.

He would rock a pair of vans because that is what happens when skaters are allowed to dress themselves. His smile would reveal pearly whites worthy of a Colgate commercial. All his friends would tease him about this trait, but that was because we were jealous and wanted our smiles to be like staring straight into the sun as well.

Emmett and I served as campus ministry interns together. We did everything as equals because we were both interns. We set up for events.

Chapter Five

We cleaned up after events. We tore down after events. We repeated the process every week.

One event was a missionary training conference. Hundreds of college students had joined us for a weekend at a campground to learn how to be effective on a mission trip. This meant every guy opted for Axe Body Spray over a locker room of cold showers. This meant every girl opted for rocking a hat with no makeup over a locker room of cold showers. This meant every person slept on a mattress so uncomfortable it might as well have been substituted for the box it came in. All of this meant hundreds of people would be sleep deprived with only one cure.

As I awoke that morning and began walking like a zombie towards a line of 150 zombies standing in front of me awaiting a cup of black gold, I saw Emmett walking away from this monstrous line with a cup of coffee in his hand. I was immediately jealous as he had clearly beaten the rush.

The pace of his walk suggested he was about to walk past me. I did not blame him. This line of people would not be over soon. As he passed me he raised his arm. Instead of taking a sip, he placed the coffee in my hand, winked his eye, and continued walking.

I do not know how early he had to get up to pull this off. I do not know how long he had to stand in line to pull this off. All I knew was this was the best cup of coffee I had ever had. But like everything, it was at a price. Emmett laid down his convenience for a friend. This is simple.

Laying down one's life for a friend can take on many facets. Sometimes it will cost reputation. Other times it will be at the burden of our bodies.

It may be as simple as giving up convenience so someone else can experience hospitality. It may be as difficult as not letting someone ignore reality so they can experience life.

Whatever the facet of laying down one's life may be, this definition of love is always applicable: Love finds a need and meets it. This is how we lay down our lives for another—we find their needs and meet them.

This is the story of the Bible. For God so loved the world, He saw the need of people and met it (John 3:16). According to Genesis, Adam and Eve, the first man and woman, were son and daughter to God. They had freedom in a garden, freedom to rule and freedom to rebel; freedom to love God and freedom to love self more than God.

This freedom gave them the dignity of choice. Pending their choice, they would become virtuous children of God or vehement creatures of iniquity.

To the demise of us all, they freely chose selfishness (Gen. 3). Into the world was born adultery, murder, lies, deceit, all kinds of evil spoken and unspeakable. This sin turned sons and daughters into creatures and strangers.

God immediately kicked Adam and Eve out of this perfect garden where they could have lived forever—because the only thing worse than a rebel is one that does not die.

A new reality was born: "For the wages of sin is death" (Rom. 6:23). Death would not be separation from God temporarily but eternally. This is fair. For if anyone wants to be god of his or her own life, heaven would be an eternal torment, as only God wears the crown.

Humanity was now doomed to death. Humanity could not remedy the situation. As I have explained before, Genesis 6 says the hearts of people were evil continually. The destination of damnation was seemingly sealed!

However, God, who made us to be His sons and daughters, wanted to change this curse. But He could not change the curse without also upholding law. Someone had committed a crime. Someone had to pay the price before reconciliation could be made.

To have a world of only mercy would create anarchy, as everyone would do what he or she thought right with no punishment of wrong. To have a world of only justice would create strangers, as everyone would do wrong because no one can truly do right!

Chapter Five

Someone would have to live the life we cannot live. Someone would have to die the death we deserve to die. Someone innocent would have to take the punishment of the guilty in order for the guilty to go free.

When Jesus preached, "Greater love has no one than this, than to lay down one's life for his friends" (John 15:13), He was not only describing what humanity must do for each other, He was telling us what He had come to earth to do for us.

Dick Brogden has preached, "The gospel is the love of God that has saved us from the wrath of God so we can enjoy the joy of God."[13]

C.S. Lewis wrote, "God became a man in order to turn creatures into sons."[14]

Malcom Muggeridge said, "Through Him, the universal becomes the particular, the imminent becomes the transcendent, the implicit becomes the explicit, always becomes now. It was for this purpose, to open a way for sinners to know God, that Jesus came among us."[15]

Real devotion entails our love for God. This is the biblical mandate. It means:

We should take every thought captive to Christ (2 Cor. 10:5).
We must not forget to fast (Matt. 6:16).
We must make disciples who make disciples (2 Tim. 2:2).
We must write God's Word on the tablets of our hearts (Prov. 7:3).
We must worship in spirit and truth (John 4:24).
We must give money we will miss to the kingdom (2 Cor. 9:7).
We must go on missions to the ends of the earth (Acts 1:8), evangelize the lost (Matt. 9:37-38), heal the sick (James 5:15), give to the poor (Prov. 19:17), and devote ourselves to prayer and the ministry of the Word (Acts 6:4).

But this real devotion of people to God can only be empowered by first believing the biblical message:

"The real devotion of God to us: Mankind needed a Savior. Jesus grabbed a cross."

Love finds a need and meets it.

Real Devotion

PART II
Faithful Practices:
Unfamiliar Whys Behind Familiar Behaviors

Real Devotion

CHAPTER SIX

Humility is a Sober Sense of Reality

OUR LAST CHAPTER EXPLAINED that love finds needs and meets them. Easier said than done! What about loving the unlovable? What about accepting the unacceptable? What about forgiving the unforgivable?

That is just regarding loving neighbors! We still have the tension of loving God, with our human hearts prone to wanting to be god of our own lives!

If we are going to love God and our neighbor, we must see them rightly. God must be seen as more than Savior. Neighbors must be viewed as more than unlovable. Faithful practices hinge on accurate perceptions. This is why God is adamant that His people humble themselves.

Humility is mentioned throughout the Bible. It is talked about concerning our relationship with God. It comes up concerning our interactions with each other. It influences how one looks in the mirror.

The great Charles Finney believed if you want to know what something is, you must first understand what it is not. This gave birth to his sermons, "True and False Conversions," "True and False Repentance," and "True and False Religion."

Using the same methodology of Mr. Finney, we want to answer what humility is by first answering what humility is not.

In high school, I ran the 300-meter hurdles in track. My coach had more than thirty years of experience. He had won numerous state championships. His athletes had won gold medals.

With a resume like this, to listen to his instruction was no less than wise. When it came to these 300-meter hurdles, he coached me on one particular principle, the starting block position. He told me over and over that what wins the 300-meter hurdles is the speed caused by zero stutter-stepping before jumping over the hurdle. The positioning of your starting blocks helps you avoid stutter-stepping because it allows you to start running from Point A and naturally reach a hurdle at Point B to jump over it at full speed without having to stutter step to prevent running into it.

Like other successful people, my coach's habits were outside the box. While every other athlete instructed by every other coach would position his starting blocks so he could have his hands on the starting line, my coach had me position my starting blocks three feet behind the starting line to help me run from Point A to Point B without stutter-stepping.

This meant that, for every race, I had to get over the mental idea I was going to lose because I was starting a yard behind everyone else. I had to trust that my coach knew what was best. And I did. I followed his methods all season long and I beat everybody, winning medal upon medal. I became district champion. I became regional champion. I broke school records.

Following his coaching took me to the state championship with the best qualifying time, which gave me the privilege of running in the best lane. With every victory I began to believe in myself.

But as human nature would have it, believing more in myself came

Chapter Six

at the expense of believing less in my coach. Where I was once the athlete that accredited victory to his instruction, I was now the athlete that accredited all success to my talent. My opinions began to outweigh his teaching.

I began to believe that team rules applied to all, but my alignment was optional. And I did not hesitate to let teammates know why I believed I was above them.

This pretentious attitude reached its pinnacle at the state championship with gold and glory on the line. With these highest stakes, I decided what got me there, or more accurately who got me there, was no longer going to help me.

I was facing off against the best of the best. I could not afford to give them a yard head start. Every inch mattered. Every second counted.

In this most important race of the season, I believed I had enough adrenaline and willpower to win on my talent, instead of my coach's instruction.

Trusting more in me than in him, I disregarded everything he had taught me and put my starting blocks on the starting line along with everyone else.

When the gun went off, I beat everyone out of the blocks because I was faster. But my timing for clearing the hurdles at full speed was now three feet off.

At the first hurdle I had to stutter step to get over it. This took me from first place to third.

At the second hurdle I had to do the same thing. Because rhythm cannot course-correct instantly, this took me from third place to fourth.

By the time I cleared the third hurdle, I was so exhausted from the six additional steps stuttering created that I dropped from fourth place into sixth.

By the time I crossed the finish line, I was dead last with my worst time of the season.

I was a winner when I believed in my coach's instruction. I was a loser when I believed in my own ability over his instruction. When I saw my coach rightly, I thought accurately of myself and the others around me, aligning with what was needed to win, resulting in victory. When I viewed my coach wrongly, I thought too much of myself and too less of others around me, disregarding what was needed to win, resulting in defeat.

This attitude is the essence of pride. Every person with pride is still living in a world built by God and surrounded by others. In a socially designed world like this, pridefully thinking too high of one's self comes at the expense of thinking too low of God and others.

Pride does not just view itself inaccurately. It comprehensively views everything else inaccurately. We see this law of pride regressing numerous people throughout the Bible.

King Nebuchadnezzar walked around the palace surveying the kingdom and began thinking to himself, "I have done this."

God heard him. Perhaps the most terrifying truth of all Scripture is that God hears our innermost thoughts about God, self, and others. Perhaps a more terrifying thought is that God Himself responds to our thoughts!

The response?

The Lord God Almighty showed King Nebuchadnezzar that he was not a god, but a finite, flawed man. God then made this finite man think like a beast (Dan. 4:33).

The king exchanged palaces for pigsties. Sophistication was replaced with sloth. Decency was turned into detriment. All of this epitomized by a king beginning to think and act less like man and more like animal!

Dr. Tim Keller exposits this principle perfectly when he says, "Every time man thinks he is more than God, he becomes less then human."[17]

Is this law not manifested throughout all the earth? Humanity knows regression caused by pride is real. Our authors attempt to cement this law into our minds by writing about it.

In *Lord of the Rings*, Sauron secures power above others at the cost of

Chapter Six

his humanity. His once great stature is reduced to a single eye void of the body it once had.

In *The Godfather*, Michael Corleone secures power by eliminating others, even family, at the cost of his humanity. His once bright future as a husband and father is reduced to an old man dying, forgotten, and alone.

In *Harry Potter*, Tom Riddle secures power above others at the cost of his humanity. His once identifiable human form is reduced to a creature-like body with skin exchanged for scales.

These consequential principles we see in fiction are a reflection of what we know to be true on earth. The regression all begins the same way. King Nebuchadnezzar first and foremost saw God wrongly. Every time a person thinks he is more than God, he becomes less than human.

Pride, however, does not end with corroding one's view of God and, as a bi-product, one's view of self. It continues into regressing one's view of others.

This is evidenced by King Saul. King Saul saw David wrongly and tried to kill him. In spite of his original call to kingship, King Saul began to behave as less than royalty by believing God too small and himself too big. He dismissed the advice of prophets, which was to dismiss the oracles of God. He called upon witches and divinations, which was to dismiss the presence of God. He ignored his responsibilities to his nation by being inactive during war, which is to dismiss the justice of God.

And, of course, he watched with envy and hate as the legend of David, his servant, grew and his own reputation decreased. "Saul has slain his thousands, and David his ten thousands," sang the crowd (1 Sam. 18:7).

Instead of rejoicing for the other person, instead of celebrating the other person, instead of empowering the other person, Saul picked up spears and threw them at the other person. He tried to kill David, his servant, his own people, his own responsibility.

He valued the loss of someone else's life over the loss of his own recognition. He preferred killing a man than watching his own reputation die!

What is the end result of a life that devalues human life?

King Saul was no longer qualified to be king. The prophet Samuel rebuked him, prophesying that he would lose his crown because he lost sight of his littleness (1 Sam. 15:17, 23)

This story communicates that leadership is retained by humility, but lost by pride. In the call of God, Saul's kingship was revoked and given to David.

In the eyes of God, losing one's character means losing one's calling. In the economy of God, once approved does not mean always approved. In the kingdom of God, no one is indispensable.

So it was with King Saul. He lost his crown and he lost his life.

This consequence began with thinking God too little and himself too big. It regressed further into thinking himself too high and his neighbor too low.

This is what pride is and does. Pride is a distorted view of what is right that interprets everything wrong. Pride views the world upside down. Everything becomes out of order. Everyone is treated with less worth than they have.

If pride leads to interpreting a world upside down, then humility must be the lens to interpreting the world right-side-up.

The evidence of humility seeing the world right-side-up is exemplified by the prophet Isaiah. In Isaiah 6:1-8, we become an audience of Isaiah before the audience of heaven.

> In the year that King Uzziah died, I saw the LORD sitting on a throne, high and lifted up and the train of His robe filled the temple. Above it stood seraphim; each one had six wings: with two he covered his face, with two he covered his feet, and with two he flew. And one cried to another and said: "Holy, holy, holy is the LORD of hosts; the

Chapter Six

whole earth is full of His glory!" And the posts of the door were shaken by the voice of him who cried out, and the house was filled with smoke. So I said: "Woe is me, for I am undone! Because I am a man of unclean lips, and I dwell in the midst of a people of unclean lips; for my eyes have seen the King, the Lord of hosts."

Then one of the seraphim flew to me, having in his hand a live coal which he had taken with the tongs from the altar. And he touched my mouth with it, and said:

"Behold, this has touched your lips; your iniquity is taken away, and your sin purged." Also I heard the voice of the Lord, saying: "Whom shall I send, and who will go for Us?" Then I said, "Here am I! Send me."

As Eli Stewart has asked, "If you could describe God in three words, what three words would you use?" Awesome? Good? Love?

The angels with a perfect vision of God and perfect proximity to God, choose one word three times over to sing of God: "Holy, holy, holy is the Lord of Hosts; the whole earth is full of His glory!"

It was a Hebrew idiom to repeat a word in order to emphasize the epitome of a quality. If a Christian was faithfully faithful, he was the epitome of everything fidelity is meant to be. Likewise, for angels to sing that God is "Holy, holy, holy" is for the entire audience of heaven to know this God is the epitome of holiness.

Holiness is not God's accessory separate from Himself. Holiness is not God's temporary attribute, coming and going when convenient. Holiness is who God intrinsically is, making everything God does holy. Because God is holy, His love is holy. His actions are holy. His wisdom is holy. His laws are holy. His governance is holy. His holy character influences His holy conduct.

People must go to God to be holy, but God is Himself holy. Always clean. Completely pure. Flawless motives. Perfectly perfect.

Not only does Isaiah hear the angels' songs to this holy God, he sees completely this holy God: "For my eyes have seen the King, the LORD of hosts!" (Isa. 6:5). God's holiness and kingship are immediately connected. There is no one like Him, therefore He is Lord. He is Lord, therefore, there is no one like Him. This is the first effect of humility in the prophet Isaiah. Before angels, he dare not speak. Before God, he dare not stand. In the awe and in his silence, he hears God clearly and sees God perfectly.

Humility, then, is a sober sense of reality. It sees everything as it should be. This humility results in a revelation of who God is.

This right revelation of God, however, does not stop Isaiah with only seeing God rightly. It progresses into seeing himself correctly, as we hear the prophet say, "Woe is me, for I am undone! Because I am a man of unclean lips."

Revelation of the holiness of God leads to revelation of the sinfulness of self, resulting in repentance. Once he sees God and, therefore, sees himself, the prophet is not bigger than his platforms, but beneath them. The prophet is not above his sermons, but subject to them. The prophet is not giving an altar call, he is responding to one.

King David needed a prophet to exclaim to him, "You are the man!" when his guilt went unknown. Isaiah had a revelation of God. This was enough to proclaim himself unclean and unworthy. For all of us who get carried away with our small titles, our temporary platforms, our feeble power, our brief popularity, we need to see God rightly to see ourselves correctly!

Important Christians know our name? But our lips are unclean! We have talent resulting in platforms? But our lips are unclean! We are moving up in authority? But our lips are unclean! We are entrusted with more responsibility? But our lips are unclean! We are advancing in scholarly knowledge? But our lips are unclean! People esteem us as holy? But our lips are unclean!

Chapter Six

We must never think God too small and ourselves too big. The Bible is clear. In spite of all our accomplishments, our righteousness is but filthy rags before a holy God.

Humility is a sober sense of reality resulting in a revelation of who God is. But humility continues with its sober sense of reality, resulting in repentance of who we are. Philip Brooks explains this process perfectly.

> The true way to be humble is not to stoop until you are smaller than yourself, but to stand at your real height against some higher nature that will show you what the real smallness of your greatest greatness is.[18]

Humility, however, does not end with seeing God and self correctly. It continues to progress into one's view of others, as we hear the prophet now say, "I am a man of unclean lips, and I dwell in the midst of a people of unclean lips."

First he saw his own sinfulness, then, in no worse comparison, he saw people's sinfulness, in need of a Savior. This is the humility of prophets. They are not less guilty than their audience. They are guilty with their audience.

Dietrich Bonhoeffer expands on this truth:

> If my sinfulness appears to me to be in any way smaller or less detestable in comparison with the sins of others, I am still not recognizing my sinfulness at all...How can I possibly serve another person in unfeigned humility if I seriously regard his sinfulness as worse than my own?[19]

In direct opposition to moral relativism that will not call anyone wrong and the humanism that calls everyone right, the prophet declares himself and his people unclean. Both deserve the wrath of a holy God upon unholy lives.

But if his revelation of humanity were to stop there, Christianity would be synonymous with cynicism. "Mankind is doomed" would merit the gospel being called anything but "good news"!

This, however, is not where the text stops. Therefore, this is not where humility stops.

Isaiah was still before the audience of God. The prophet, who was most certainly between shock and awe before His holiness, overheard the voice of God: "I heard the voice of the LORD, saying: "Whom shall I send, and who will go for Us?" (Isa. 6:8).

We must not miss what is happening here. The love of God longs to save humanity from the wrath our rebellion has wrought. God will not watch in dismay. He must save the humanity that cannot save itself!

Our hands are not clean. Our hearts are not pure. Our souls are lifted to vanity. We swear deceitfully. We cannot ascend the hill of the Lord! This makes us doomed to live without God forever, for unclean people and a holy God cannot dwell together.

But this King of Kings chose to empty Himself. He left perfect heaven to be born on imperfect earth. He came to live the life we could never live in order to die the death we should have died.

Sin merits punishment. Someone must pay. Jesus joyfully chose to grab the punishment of a cross and ascend the hill of the Lord for us! (Ps.24:3-4).

We can be sons and daughters because Jesus became a stranger! We can be forgiven because Jesus became our debt! We can be alive because Jesus became our death!

The heart of God is missional! He left comfort for a cross. He went out to seek and save the lost! This is the good news of the gospel: Humanity was doomed to death, so God sent Himself to save us!

In this audience with our missional God, the prophet heard the Godhead inquire, "Who will share this good news for us?"

Isaiah, after seeing God rightly, now sees himself and others rightly. With this sobriety he willingly responds, "Here am I! Send me" (Isa.

Chapter Six

6:8) .

Do you see the progression of humility? Humility is a sober sense of reality, resulting in a revelation of who God is. Humility continues with its sober sense of reality, resulting in repentance of who we are.

But the fruition of humility is not over with mere repentance of self. Humility continues with its sober sense of reality, resulting in responsibility for whom we are around.

Isaiah knew he was surrounded by sinners who must bow to the Lord and must hear why! He would not let prayer be a substitute for obedience. He must go! He would not merely celebrate those in the work of the Lord while he did not work. He must go! He would not settle for right theology and absent methodology. He must go! He would not wait for the Lord to specifically address Him by voice or vision. People are unholy and God is worthy. He volunteered because he must go!

As he went, he did not exchange the declaration of the gospel for the demonstration of the gospel. He made his holiness a light, but not at the absence of his words to be a voice. He lived for Christ, but he did not neglect defining Christ:

> Behold, God is my salvation, I will trust, and will not be afraid, for the Lord God is my strength and my song, and He has become my salvation (Isa. 12:2, ESV).

> He was wounded for our transgressions (Isa. 53:5).

> For unto us a Child is born, unto us a Son is given, and the government shall be upon His shoulder, and His name will be called Wonderful, Counselor, Mighty God, Everlasting Father, Prince of Peace (Isa. 9:6).

Do you see the progression of Isaiah's revelation? Humility is a sober sense of reality, resulting in a revelation of who God is. Humility is a sober sense of reality, resulting in repentance of who we are. Humility is a sober sense of reality, resulting in responsibility for whom we are around.

"Holy, holy, holy is the LORD of hosts...Woe is me...I am a man of unclean lips, and I dwell in the midst of a people of unclean lips...Here am I! Send me."

Humility progresses from revelation of God, to a repenting spirit, to a responsible spirit.

This must mean that if we have not developed a repenting spirit, we have not yet seen God. This must mean if we have not developed a responsible spirit, we have not yet repented!

Have we seen God's holiness that makes angels sing? Have we seen God's lordship that makes prophets repent? Have we seen the world's uncleanness that makes us volunteer, "Here I am, Send me"?

CHAPTER SEVEN

Feelings Follow Actions

WE HAVE DISCOVERED humility is a sober sense of reality, beginning with a revelation of who God is, continuing into repentance of who we are, and finding its fruition in responsibility to whom we are around.

Although real responsibility could contain its own book's worth of truth and application, it begins with a real devotion to obey God, especially when one does not feel like it! This thought process is counter-cultural to how our society behaves today, but it is this thought process of Jesus and this culture of the cross we must examine now.

When we begin to study relationships, we quickly discover that the romantic ones tend to begin the same way. In middle school, hormones take over and young people who cannot vote, cannot see R-rated movies, cannot drive themselves to a date, and (generally speaking) do not work and, therefore, cannot afford to date, decide it's time to "go out" with someone.

This decision could be attributed to too much Justin Bieber. Or, if you grew up in the Nineties, too much NSYNC. Or if you grew up in the Eighties, too much New Kids on the Block, who had a bunch of hits, and Chinese food that made you sick.

But at its foundation, people begin to date because a guy feels a girl is attractive, and a girl feels the guy is cool. The guy asks the girl to "go out," although in middle school you really do not go anywhere.

A "date" in middle school usually means sitting in a lunch room that smells like too much Axe Body Spray with hundreds of other preteens, all hopped up on Sprite Remix as they discuss the latest episode of *Degrassi High*.

Or, if you grew up in the Nineties, all hopped up on Surge while discussing the latest episode of *Saved by the Bell*. Or, if you grew up in the Eighties, all hopped up on Orange Julius while discussing the latest episode of *The Wonder Years*.

Whatever decade it might be, one thing remains true: Middle school relationships begin with feelings which lead to action.

In high school, this foundation for romantic relationship continues. A guy feels a girl is attractive. A girl feels the guy is cool. The entire process repeats itself, but this time without parental chaperones, more limousine rides, and, ideally, less Axe Body Spray.

This process of feelings leading to action continues into college and adult romance. What we feel creates what we do, leading to a culture where feeling is the foundation of relationship.

This culture seems to work at first because when a relationship begins, everyone is on his or her best behavior. The girl dresses up with her finest jewelry and make up. The guy cleans everything he owns and spares no expense with the dates.

The girl may name drop something or someone to sound connected. The guy will attempt to sound intelligent by using a big word he learned earlier when he randomly opened the dictionary for the first time ever.

Everyone is on his or her best behavior when the relationship is new and feelings are new. But what happens when the relationship becomes familiar and feelings wane?

Chapter Seven

The cultural narrative of our time insists feelings are the foundation to any action, including, but not limited to, starting or ending a relationship. Our society says, "Do what you feel," which, of course, implies, "Do not do what you do not feel." Believing to act on your feelings is to fulfill yourself, but to act against your feelings is to betray yourself! When the going gets tough, we are trained to believe it is authentic to get out. One disagreement means a relationship is over. One fight means faithfulness can be removed. Any tension in a relationship means it is time for transition out of the relationship.

But do you see how this habit of feelings leading to action not only affects the relationships of a person with people, but a person with God?

Make no mistake, the feelings of Jesus for us is not the problem. "For the joy set before Him He endured the cross" (Heb. 12:2). "For God so loved the world that He gave His only begotten Son" (John 3:16). "Christ Jesus, who, being in the form of God, did not consider it robbery to be equal with God, but made Himself of no reputation" (Phil. 2: 5-7). His actions and feelings are the same from one day to the next. But our emotions are the ones that toss like waves. Our feelings are the vapors here one day and gone the next. Our conditional commitment and love of God is the problem!

How many people have felt a fire for God at conferences where we feel His presence, only to leave a conference behind and, by choice, leave His presence behind?

How many people have felt strongly to pledge their obedience to God in public with friends, only to compromise in private when no audience means no feelings?

How many of us pledge to read the Bible, only to stop reading the Bible when what it says convicts us?

We justify this lack of obedience to God, believing the cultural narrative, "Do what you feel," but, "Do not do what you do not feel," as if reading the Bible when you do not feel like it is legalistic and wrong; as if one has to feel love for an enemy before giving love to one's enemy;

as if missions hinges on emotion instead of a verse; as if discipleship depends on our convenience instead of God's command; as if we have the right to rebel against God before we feel like obeying God; as if we can say,"No, King Jesus," and still be Christian!

The Lord is not a stranger to us. But with this behavior of waiting on right feelings to lead to right actions, we become strangers to God!

Let us be honest. What Christian can afford to wait until they feel like obeying God to obey God? The commands of the Lord are already inconvenient and uncomfortable!

"Go therefore and make disciples of all the nations...teaching them to observe all things that I have commanded you" (Matt. 28:19-20).

Go? Make disciples? Teach them to observe everything Jesus commanded? Including the most difficult commands like:

"Love your enemies" (Matt. 5:44).

"In honor giving preference to one another" (Rom. 12:10).

"Forgiving one another" (Col. 3:13).

"Pray without ceasing" (1 Thess. 5:17).

"You shall lay up these words of mine in your heart and in your soul...speaking of them when you sit in your house, when you walk by the way, when you lie down, and when you rise up"(Deut. 11:18-19).

"Do not look at people lustfully" (Matt. 5:28, *my paraphrase*).

Furthermore, let us not forget the prerequisite to follow Jesus that no person readily feels like obeying: "If anyone desires to come after Me, let him deny himself, and take up his cross daily, and follow Me" (Luke 9:23).

With absolute clarity and making no apologies, the commands of Christ call for actions that do not readily align with our feelings. We may have begun our relationship with Jesus because of feelings that led to actions. But if we are going to continue in our relationship with Jesus, we have to obey Him with actions even when His commands evoke uncomfortable feelings.

If I obey God only when I feel like it, I will always rebel against

Chapter Seven

Him. If I love Him only when I feel like it, I will always leave Him. If I abide in Him only when I feel the moment is right, I will always be wrong. If right actions hinge first on experiencing right feelings, then the world would have no martyrs, the gospel would have reached no Gentiles, and Christ would have no Christians!

To follow Jesus only when we feel like it is to fail. Christians are the people who obey God especially when they do not feel like obeying God because God is God and they are not.

Jeremiah told God he did not want to be His prophet anymore. The nation he loved hated him and his God. He felt rejected. He wanted to resign. But he continued the action of preaching, citing God's word as a fire in his bones (Jer. 20:9).

David felt like he could kill his enemy, King Saul, in the darkness of a cave with no witnesses around. He chose the action of mercy, settling for taking a garment instead of a life, and he still repented (1 Sam. 24:6).

Elisabeth Elliot watched a village turn her missionary husband into a martyr. Her response was to "love her enemies" and "pray for those who persecute you" by continuing to serve that village as a widowed missionary with her fatherless daughter (Matt. 5:44).

Do we see the reality of our "feeling only" application? If we wait to feel like obeying Jesus before we obey Jesus, we will never obey Jesus! Relationships begin with feelings leading to action. But relationships continue and Christianity is built on feelings that follow action.

Love is a force more than it is a feeling. Believing first produces seeing second. We must read the Bible in order to want to read the Bible. We must pray to God to want to pray to God. We have to go on a mission trip to feel like going on a mission trip. We need to volunteer to make disciples before we feel called to make disciples. We have to die to self to be alive in Christ.

Christianity is following Jesus when we do not want to follow Jesus, in order to follow Jesus.

Feelings follow action.

Real Devotion

CHAPTER EIGHT

Prayer is Not About What You Do, But Whose You Are

TO SUMMARIZE OUR LAST CHAPTER: The secret to faithful practices is obeying Jesus, especially when we do not feel like it. Through repetition of this discipline, feelings will follow action.

In these next two chapters, we will look at two specific actions, investigating why prayer is the empowerment behind any action, and why we must let no action be disconnected from our Savior.

Multiple sermons, Bible classes and book volumes have been composed on prayer. The topics on prayer have covered why prayer must be persistent, the mystery of how it all works, the reasons why prayer is unanswered, the necessity of humility, and the effect of prayer on people and nations. The list is vast because God is vast.

With that said, this is a chapter, not a book, on prayer. Within all the vastness of prayer, we want to look at why we can talk to the God of heaven and earth, who uses prayer to empower any action.

Allow me, then, to start with a story.

Kuren was a student in our college ministry. He had bright, blonde hair and wore a perpetual tan. His vocabulary was primarily composed of the words "dude" and "gnarly," and the occasional phrase, "legalize it." Without him telling us his origin story, we immediately knew he was from California.

He was a talented young man we had the honor of calling friend. He went to the university to study golf, something he had played since his youth.

Kuren made his high school cash working on one of California's finest golf courses. This led to numerous experiences that turned into numerous stories, this being one of them.

He spent his days selling drinks to thirsty golfers, washing golf carts, and helping people improve their swing. His instruction was more than welcome. While most golfers scored triple digits, he was in the low seventies on bad days.

One day, Kuren was going through the routine of closing down greens when a golf cart headed to hole one, as if to begin the day while everyone was ending theirs. Golfers who believed course hours were relative was a normal occurrence, followed by the phrase no customer likes to hear, "I am sorry, but we are closed."

What then transpired was an abnormal occurrence as this late customer was quite familiar.

The driver pulled up, strutted out of his golf cart, grabbed his clubs like he owned the place, and began walking towards a waiting Kuren. As he moved closer, the man removed his shades and hat, causing Kuren to drop his jaw and forget the course had a closing time.

This is because Kuren found himself standing face-to-face with a famous actor who goes by the name Will Smith, an actor made popular by the show *Fresh Prince of Bel-Air* and movies like *Independence Day,* which nearly everyone remembers, as well as *After Earth,* which everyone wants to forget.

Kuren let him stay and play, proving opened doors really are about who you know, or more accurately, who knows you.

As they went from one hole to another, Will Smith asked Kuren for

Chapter Eight

golf tips of which he was happy to provide.

"How far do your feet need to be apart when you drive the ball?"

"What do you do with your hands during a swing?"

"How do you know which club to use at any given time?"

Kuren then asked this Hollywood star for acting tips for the drama class he was enrolled in, of which the famous thespian was happy to oblige.

"How do you make an audience laugh?"

"What do you do to memorize lines?"

"How do you develop chemistry with other actors?"

Although this story is uncommon, the interaction is quite common. If you need to become a better golfer, when you come across a golfing instructor, you are going to ask him questions about your swing, not how to cry on cue for cameras and lights.

If you need to become a better actor, when you come across a movie star, you are going to ask him questions about transforming into a role, not how to take five strokes off your game. This is because "how to" questions are reserved for those who have demonstrated success in a specific field.

When we look at the life of Jesus, there are limitless "how to" questions we could ask Him as He has demonstrated success in various fields, including, but not limited to, raising the dead, loving neighbors, loving enemies, defeating the works of the devil, and conquering the grave. To name a few.

And yet, the disciples of Jesus asked Him only one "how to" question within their three-year span with Him.

"Now it came to pass, as He was praying in a certain place, when He ceased, that one of His disciples said to Him, 'Lord, teach us (how) to pray'" (Luke 11:1, *words in parentheses mine*).

Of all the "how to" questions one could ask Jesus, why is it in three brief yet full years, the disciples who saw Jesus more than anyone, who were taught by Jesus more than anyone, who were with Jesus more than anyone, asked Jesus this one "how to" question?

They saw His hands heal. They heard His sermons which had authority. They watched His righteous anger throw tables around in a den of thieves. They experienced His forgiveness. They heard His voice quiet storms. They listened to His stories illuminate reality. They watched Him lead imperfect people in a perfect way. But it seems the ability and the habit that intrigued them most was His prayer life.

Often the gospels tell us Jesus withdrew to lonely places to pray (Luke 5:16). Luke 11 begins by telling us He was praying in a certain place. He prayed without His disciples, as He would depart for hours at a time to be with His Father. He prayed with His disciples and they experienced an intimacy with God they had never known before.

These prayers of Jesus must have shaken the disciples as only heaven can do when it comes down to visit earth. Witnessing this prayer life, they became convinced His time with God is what influenced His power with people. Because He talked long with God, He could hold the attention of humanity. Because He was filled with heaven, He could cast out hell. Because He knew the will of God, He could call disorder into order. Because He prayed, He could confidently claim the promises of God. Because He prayed, He could unveil the mysteries of God.

They believed His prayer was the secret to His power, therefore, prayer must be the secret to any power. This meant they had to do everything possible to learn how to speak with God, so they, like Jesus, might bring heaven to earth.

With this understanding, they asked Jesus, "Lord, teach us to pray."

Is it not interesting that, when Jesus was asked by His disciples, "Teach us how to pray," He did not begin with "Our Lord," or "Our Bridegroom," or by saying "Our Friend"— all of which would have been an accurate assessment of God. Rather, Jesus said in Luke 11:2, "When you pray, say: Our Father in heaven, hallowed be Your name," which means, "God our Father, be known for who you are."

Of all the names of God, why does Jesus make it imperative for us

Chapter Eight

to start prayer by saying, "Our Father in heaven"?

Growing up as a kid, there was a television show which everyone watched. It was called "Mighty Morphin' Power Rangers."

Not to be confused with "Mighty Morphin' Alien Rangers," or "Power Rangers Zeo," or "Power Rangers Turbo," or "Power Rangers in Space," where every franchise goes to die, or "Power Rangers Time Force," or "Power Rangers Wild Force," or "Power Rangers Mega Force," or even "Power Rangers Super Mega Force." Clearly, nothing tells children something is new and worth watching like replacing one word with a synonymous word.

The show was about good guys getting into karate fights with bad guys from alternate dimensions in order to save the world. The natural bi-product of this was every kid picking a fight with every other kid.

For instance, while playing outside with the rest of the neighborhood one day, my little six-year-old brother got into a heated argument with a kid eight years older than himself down the street. My brother was scrawny. He probably weighed twenty pounds and was as tall as a fire hydrant. The kid he was arguing with was older, fifty pounds heavier, and, without a doubt, tougher. The word in the neighborhood was this kid had a tattoo of a mermaid on his back, and she had a tattoo of him on her back, and you just don't mess with a guy like that.

This infamous bully was making fun of my little brother for being little. He, of course, did not like that. To retaliate, my brother looked him straight in the eye and said, "You will not make fun of me ever again because I am going to get my big brother, and he is going to beat you up while I steal your girlfriend and watch the fight!" He then kicked over this kid's bicycle, hopped on his tricycle, and rode all the way home, yelling for me to save him.

This was my little brother, the shortest kid on the block. Lighter than a softball. And yet, he stood up to a giant who was bigger, stronger, and tougher than him.

What motivates this audacious courage? What influences this

confidence? My little brother, Andrew, knew I was his older brother. He viewed me as stronger, taller, and tougher than anybody out there. But more than just what I could do, it was who I was to him that instilled the confidence to pick a fight.

When we believe we are connected to someone powerful, we act with the belief that our relationship with him or her gives validation to what we can do.

Do you see how this relates to prayer?

We have grown up in a self-made culture where what we do determines what we get. If I work hard, I can get a better education. If I get a better education, I can get a better job. If I get a better job, my children can have a better education.

Then the cycle of getting the best for myself repeats itself.

But Jesus did not describe prayer in a self-made culture dependent on what we do. He told His disciples to pray by beginning, "Our Father," which is the vocabulary of family culture. In a family, if children ask a father for anything, the answer is not determined by what they do. It is determined by whose they are.

As Tim Keller has said, "The only person who can disturb a king at three in the morning for a glass of water is a child of the king!"[20]

Because God is Father, our relationship with Him gives validity to what we can do! Telling people they can pray to God by saying, "Our Father," was not the message of the day! It moved prayer away from the atmosphere of personal accomplishments into the atmosphere of personal relationship. A "do-and-receive" mentality was being replaced with a "know-and-be-known" mentality.

This was entirely contrary to the culture of the time that made religion inaccessible. If you wanted to go to God, you went to the priest, who then went on your behalf to God. The priest was the one who did the work of religion and, therefore, got the rewards of religion: the presence of the Lord.

This meant that if "priest" did not appear on your tax return, you

Chapter Eight

did not know how to pray and could not pray. If this thinking applied to our world today, it would mean only the pastor can meet with the Lord of heaven and earth. The businessman can have no access to God. The college student can only dream of catching the ear of heaven. The child cannot run into the arms of Jesus!

In that culture, God is too holy to come close. He is too awful for us to stay long in His presence. Stories were told throughout the centuries of God coming down to a mountain once, and telling a nation that if they went near His fiery presence, they would die (Ex.19:12). Going to God was a privilege held by a few priests based on what they had done in education and vocation. For Jesus to now say you can pray by calling God "Father" was a welcomed message to weary people. You can now meet with Him!

Dick Foth described this before-and-after experience brilliantly. He said that when you are a toddler, you are always looking up to your father. He stands what seems like fifteen-feet high to a toddler who is three-feet tall! That is a highly, inaccessible giant.

Can you imagine what it would be like for a small person to interact with a giant?

The giant would come home from a long day of work. He would ask the toddler if he has cleaned his room. The toddler, who does not want to get in trouble with someone so huge, would wisely reply while looking up, "Well, no sir, but I was just on my way to do it."

The toddler would have a vertical relationship with the giant!

Every action would be about staying out of trouble under the watch of a powerful giant, or being good in order to get help from this powerful giant. But when this giant dad comes home and lays his body on the floor, what happens? His toddler children rush his giant body! They climb all over him! They play all over him! And he plays with them!

When the giant lays his body down, the vertical becomes horizontal and the horizontal is now accessible![21]

By claiming God is Father, Jesus is letting every person know that

God is accessible! The vertical God the Son has come down to earth to live horizontally as the Son of Man among His people!

Because of Jesus, His life, death, and resurrection, we can now have access to God as children with the privilege of calling Him our Father. This truth was revolutionary then. It is revolutionary still! Prayer is not about what you do, but whose you are!

Because we are God's children, we have access to God!

CHAPTER NINE

Never Let Serving God Get in the Way of Knowing God

CONTINUING OUR LOOK into faithful practices, we must admit there is much one can and should do for God, and much one can and will experience.

Prayer should be a daily discipline. We will see answers, but they must not go to our head. We will see no answers; these must not go to our head. We will carry crosses for Jesus. This action will lead to an Easter morning! But other times we will feel like it is just leading to a bigger grave.

We will give God the service of ministry, be it making disciples, participating in missions, giving to missions, preaching, teaching, and the like. We will see success. We will experience suffering. This is why it becomes imperative for no action or result of any faithful practice to be disconnected from our Savior.

Let us look at why serving God can make us lose focus on God, and what we can do to get back to Him.

For as long as I can remember, I have always wanted to have a missionary kid. This is the default name given to children of missionary parents. Missionary kids experience the world unlike their peer counterparts. Where most children know one culture, these children can know multiple. Where most children never leave America or even their home state, these children experience more travel in their childhood then most people do in their lifetimes.

Furthermore, where most children rarely experience the inside of a worship service, these children grow accustomed to worship services. They are as common as recess.

For the longest time, we waited to have a missionary kid of our own—a child to love, a child to raise, a child who could experience the adventure that is living for Jesus. For the longest time this child never came. This led my wife and I to become foster parents, as this book has mentioned. Our first placement became our first missionary kid, a two-year old little girl named K. Her sassiness and assimilation to Chi Alpha culture was a unique combination.

One night, she did not want to finish her bath by actually bathing. She preferred to just play in the water with whatever came to her imagination.

I said, "K, you need to use your soap, sweetheart."

But to try and defer me from her task, she dropped the soap from her hands, raised both her arms to the sky, closed her eyes, and began saying, "Jesus, Jesus," with a smile on her face and one eye open to see if I was paying attention.

I responded, "Baby girl, I love you. But you cannot fake-worship Jesus to get out of responsibility."

My wife and I were dedicated to serving this precious little girl. We would make her meals, buy her clothes, get her from one meeting to another, as foster children are never short on appointments.

We were dedicated to finding friends for K. I would take her to the park to meet new people. We would host play dates where the children of our other missionary friends could spend time with her. We would tell people about K. We wanted to make people aware of the ministry

Chapter Nine

of foster care, believing through demonstration and declaration the fatherless and motherless would soon have parents and homes.

I would do all these things for K. Every day was filled from sunup to sundown with activities!

One day stands out in particular. It was an afternoon like any other. The appointments and play dates were over. Dinner and bath time were up. Story time and bed were soon to follow.

As K was coloring in the dining room, I was moving from one room to another taking care of multiple tasks at once. I walked past her to check on the food in the kitchen. I walked past her to the library to prepare for sermon writing later that evening. I walked past her to the living room to bring some order to the chaos play dates bring. I walked past her to the hallway to take a call from a student who needed something. I walked past her to the door to answer a missionary who needed something. I walked past her back to the kitchen to check on the food.

As I walked past her this time, with my mind seemingly on the current task and the next task all at once, I felt my arm being grasped by a small, little hand. Before I could turn my eyes to meet hers, I heard her small, little voice command, "Daddy, sit. Just be wit' me."

I do not remember what the people on the phone wanted. I cannot recall what the sermon preparation was about. The living room stayed a mess until she went to sleep. I am pretty sure dinner was burnt that night. I do not remember how long I sat at the table and just colored with her. But I do remember wishing the moment could last forever.

As I reflect on that moment that seems to stand still in time, I am filled with revelation of what is true. To serve her was not equivalent to being with her. To introduce new friends to her was not equivalent to being her friend. To tell people about her was not equivalent to talking with her myself. It was one thing to work for K. It was something altogether different to be with K.

As we survey life with God, is the same revelation not also true for us?

The Bible is filled with language from a God who does not merely want to be around us, but a part of us! This loving God declares to an unborn people, "Before I formed you in the womb I knew you" (Jer. 1:5). The distraught God calls out in the garden to a hiding humanity, "Where are you?" (Gen. 3:9).

The story continues with God creating the way to His people. "For God so loved the world that He gave His only begotten Son" (John 3:16). The story ends with what this God has always wanted:

> Then I saw "a new heaven and a new earth," for the first heaven and the first earth had passed away, and there was no longer any sea. I saw the Holy City, the new Jerusalem, coming down out of heaven from God, prepared as a bride beautifully dressed for her husband. And I heard a loud voice from the throne saying, "Look! God's dwelling place is now among the people, and He will dwell with them. They will be His people, and God Himself will be with them and be their God" (Rev. 21:1-3, NIV).

Yes, we must give back to the God who gave all. Yes, we must serve the Jesus who saved us. But, no, serving God does not equate to being with God!

It can become our tendency to serve Jesus, believing it equates to being with Him. It can become our tendency to introduce new people to Jesus, believing it equates to abiding with Him. It can become our tendency to tell people about Jesus, believing it equates to praying with Him. But we must make no mistake, it is not our primary purpose to work for Jesus. It is our primary purpose to be with Jesus!

Our primary purpose is not a place, a position, a platform, or a people group. Our primary purpose is to be with the person of Jesus, that we may gain the glory of the Lord Jesus, that we may take hold of Him who is eternal life, that His eternal glory may perfect us, confirm

Chapter Nine

us, strengthen us, establish us, that He will be our God and we will be His people.

How easy it is to let activity avert us from this glorious purpose! We can have this nasty habit of letting serving God replace knowing God, especially when this service leads to success or suffering.

Many characters within the Bible have stories of service leading to less of God or more of God. Simply look at King Saul, who failed under success, and John the Baptist, who triumphed under suffering.

When we first meet Saul, he is not a king, nor does he believe he is qualified to be. We meet a man in full consciousness of his own littleness.

In his first conversation with Samuel the prophet, we hear Saul speak of himself, "Am I not a Benjamite, of the smallest of the tribes of Israel, and my family the least of all the families of the tribe of Benjamin?" (1 Sam. 9:21).

As he is declared the next king of Israel, we find him not eagerly awaiting the throne, but hiding behind suitcases (1 Sam 10:22). This is a man who does not want to be seen. This is a man who does not want to be known. This is a man who does not believe he is qualified to rule.

But what happened to him as he served God? Under his leadership, a nation experienced victories won and territories gained. Under his leadership, people followed his command and revered his name. Somewhere in this process of serving God and gaining notoriety, this man lost sight of his own littleness. Waiting on God for a prophet to give God's command was replaced with making his own commands. Complete obedience was replaced with manipulative obedience—he obeyed God his way instead of God's way. Sanctification was replaced with sorcery (1 Sam. 28:7). Humility was replaced with haughtiness, and in the end, the man who was called to be king was dismissed, as the Lord then sought out for Himself a person after His own heart "because you (Saul) have not kept what the LORD commanded you" (1 Sam. 13:14).

King Saul's big accomplishments made him lose sight of his littleness. He forgot that the Lord builds the house. He forgot accomplishments are not by might, nor by strength, but by God's Spirit. In the process of serving the Lord, he saw success. In knowing success he stopped knowing the Lord. In forgetting the Lord, he lost character. In losing godly character, he lost God's call.

The Lord then found a new king for Israel.

If we, like King Saul, are losing our character because of our success, how do we move from serving God to knowing God again?

We begin by remembering service is not synonymous with surrender. Do we have altar calls before we ask people to come to the altars? Do we pray for ourselves before we pray for people? Do we seek counsel before we give it? Do we read the Bible looking for God instead of looking for a sermon? Do we write messages for us instead of an audience? Do we go to church to find God instead of looking for a platform? Do we lead ourselves to Jesus before we lead others to responsibility?

Serving God can produce success, but let us never let serving God get in the way of knowing God. Although serving the Lord can produce success, it can also produce suffering, which can also impede the knowledge of the Lord. But it does not have to!

This was the case of John the Baptist. John's ministry began with glory. From the womb, it was prophesied he would prepare the way of the Lord (Luke 1:13-17). At the sound of the mother of Jesus, he kicked for joy! He spent his youth in the wilderness, misunderstood by men but understood by God. He made disciples who would go on and make disciples. He baptized many people, but only John the Baptist can claim he baptized the very Son of God!

In the process of this baptism of Christ, another supernatural occurrence happened. He heard the very voice of God! "This is My Beloved Son, in whom I am well pleased" (Matt. 3:17). God the Son confirmed by God the Father in John's very presence! There is no greater apologetic than experience!

His sound theology is confirmed in his preaching, "Behold! the Lamb of God who takes away the sin of the world!" (John 1:29).

Chapter Nine

In the process of serving God, he knew God, and his ministry knew success. But through the displeasure of a sinner in royalty who did not enjoy having her sin called out, this prophet found himself in a prison (Luke 3:19-20). In this prison, it became clear evil had conspired against him with one ambition, to silence his voice through death.

Doing the right thing brought upon John the wrong circumstance. He had fought for good, but evil had triumphed.

In prison he called for his disciples to visit Jesus and ask one question: "Are you the Coming One? Or do we look for another?" (Luke 7:19).

How does a man go from exclaiming, "Behold the Lamb of God!" to inquiring, "Are you the Son of God?"

Look for a moment in a mirror. In moments of suffering, have we ever looked to Jesus to inquire, "Is my cross worth Your crown?" John's response shows us the difference between prophets and pagans. When one's world is falling apart, the pagan exclaims, "There is no god," but the prophet inquires of God!

Is this not Jacob running for his life, yet grabbing onto the Angel to not let go until he is blessed? Is this not Moses, carrying the burden of leading a nation, not moving a muscle unless a cloud guides by day and a pillar of fire by night? Is this not Peter, having left all, inquiring of Jesus to whom else shall they go? Only the One with the crown has the words of eternal life.

Jesus, being good, did not leave his prophet unanswered. He told the disciples to answer the question, "Are you the Coming One?" with this: "The blind receive sight, the lame walk, those who have leprosy are cleansed, the deaf hear, the dead are raised, and the good news is proclaimed to the poor. Blessed is anyone who does not stumble on account of Me" (Luke 7:22-23).

What is the Christ saying to suffering circumstances? Life is guilty, but the Lord is innocent. The physically dead meet Jesus and come alive. The spiritually dead meet Jesus and come alive. The bad news of circumstances does not detract from the good news: Jesus came to save sinners!

The gospel has an eternal impact beyond any temporal malady. Yes, life is guilty, but Jesus exchanged His innocence for our guilt. Yes, we will experience loss, but it does not stop Jesus from being the life. Yes, life is filled with death, but Jesus is the resurrection.

Temporal trial does not erase the absolute gospel. Jesus who knew no sin became sin so we can become the righteousness of God (2 Cor. 5:21).

If service has not saved us from suffering, how do we move from serving God to knowing God again?

Like prophets, we inquire of God. Perhaps God will answer. Or perhaps He will point us to the Bible, the narrative of which talks less about what our service should deserve and more about the gospel we will never deserve. Our service is filthy rags. His service washed us white as snow. Our names are vapors, here one day and gone the next. His name makes every knee bow and tongue confess. Our hearts are prone to selfishness. His heart knew no selfishness, and became selfishness, so we can become the righteousness of God. Our joy is in grabbing crowns. His joy was in grabbing a cross so we may grab a crown.

Here is a simple sentence to become our battle cry when battles make us cry, and when territory gained tempts us to have humility lost:

Never let serving God get in the way of knowing God.

CHAPTER TEN

Discipline, Desire, Delight

WE HAVE COME to the final chapter. We have learned unfamiliar "whys" behind familiar beliefs. We have learned unfamiliar "whys" behind familiar behaviors. Hopefully, all of this has created a greater love for the Jesus devoted to us, and instilled in us a greater desire to give real devotion to Jesus.

This brings us to an application that can exist well beyond the closing of this book, influencing our days and changing our lives until Jesus comes back.

My first year in missions was spent overseas. My wife and I had joined a team on a ten-month assignment to plant a college ministry in the country of Kazakhstan in 2009. During these ten months, we quickly discovered these Russian-speaking Kazaks loved Americans. If you were in a taxi ride, which was basically Uber with a haggling system for the consumer and no certification requirements for the driver, the driver would discover you were American from your accent and, with no regard to political sensitivity, like a Southern family around the Thanksgiving table, he would look you in the eye through his rearview mirror to say, "Obama, yes! (with a thumbs up), Bush, no! (with a thumbs down)."

If you walked onto the campuses of Kazakhstan, every student would identify you as American based on your diversity of looks. They would then flash two thumbs up and utter two words of peacemaking in their thick accents: "Star Wars."

Because you were American, everyone wanted to talk to you and express appreciation to you. You received better service at restaurants. Stores gave you discounts. People were more pleasant.

In this context, it became easy for us to believe our American nationality was the ticket to whatever we wanted.

One team member, let's call him "Jimmy" (which is not his name), took this national entitlement belief to the extreme.

His plane ticket home was set for August. His current visa was expiring in July. He had to pay to renew his visa to stay legally, and then fly home. Or, he thought, if he just used his pen to make the 7 for July look like an 8 for August, it would look like his visa did not need to be renewed. He could pay zero dollars, and then fly home.

He believed, because he was American, his host country would be none the wiser. He believed, because he was American, that if his forgery was discovered, he would be dismissed with a reprimand at best. After all, he believed, his nationality was the ticket to whatever he wanted.

He forged the numbers on his government visa. He went to the airport to fly home. A few hours later, our team received a call from authorities about our American who was in custody until he made bail.

Jimmy quickly discovered that no matter what we thought about our nation, being American was not a ticket to whatever we wanted. It did not set us up for default success. It did not entitle us to break rules without repercussion. It did not mean we were free from conditions and consequences.

This mindset of nationality being a ticket to whatever is wanted was the mindset of Israel in Bible times. They grew to believe their

Chapter Ten

nationality, which associated them with God, equaled salvation. They could be unfaithful to God. They could live by their own rules. They could neglect His conditional promises. They believed they could do all of this and their souls would have no consequences.

This led to Old Testament prophets describing the nation as a vine, but a degenerate one. They were meant to have salvation. They were meant to be a conduit for the world's salvation. But they put their hope in things less than Jesus, and themselves became less.

With the context of a nation believing its nationality entitled them to salvation, Jesus preached in John 15:1, "I am the true vine," creating a contrast between what they wanted to believe and what they needed to believe.

William Barclay exposits Christ's preaching this way:

> Jesus was laying it down that not Jewish blood but faith in Him was the way to God's salvation. No external qualification can set a man right with God, only the friendship of Jesus can do that.[22]

Just as the people of Israel believed their souls' salvation was in a nationality, as opposed to the person of Jesus, Christians are in danger of believing their ministry's salvation is in a method or system or talent or team, as opposed to the person of Jesus!

Whether we are leading large groups or small groups, whether we are in ministry as vocation or as a volunteer, we are tempted to believe leadership replication is a matter of leadership curriculum, so we ask, "What are you teaching?" We are inclined to believe ministry growth is a matter of ministry experience, so we ask, "What are you doing?" We are taught to believe ministry attraction is a matter of excellence, so we ask, "How are you performing?" We are influenced to believe ministry retention is a matter of political correctness, so we ask, "What are you preaching?" Or, more accurately, "What are you not preaching?"

All the while Jesus promises in John 15:5, "I am the vine, you are the branches; He who abides in Me and I in Him, bears much fruit, for without Me you can do nothing."

This should make it abundantly clear to anyone who confesses real devotion to Jesus that the primary question for a ministry's salvation is not, "What are you doing?" but, "How is your abiding in Jesus?"

This is what John 15:5 is about—abiding. The word literally means to remain, to dwell with, to make your home with. Simply put, to abide is to spend extravagant time with someone. Therefore, to abide in Jesus is to spend extravagant time with Jesus.

This is more than two hours once a week with Jesus at a large group. This is more than three minutes a day in intercession. This is more than being with Jesus exclusively in social settings, for whose lover or Lord is limited to social settings?

When it comes to John 15:5, our problem is not that we do not believe it, but that we believe too much in ourselves. Our unbelief in the glorious promise of John 15 has nothing to do with thinking abiding in Jesus is impossible, but obstinately believing abiding in Jesus is unnecessary!

This is the epitome of Christian narcissism, the belief that we can do much for God without God. Perhaps a quick recall of the gospel we believe may help us remember how obstinate our Christian narcissism is.

Christians believe God existed before anything. By Himself He created everything, including humankind, in His image to be His people. We rebelled after being tempted by the devil disguised as a snake.

God kicked us out of a perfect garden so we would not become immortal rebels from the fruit of a tree. Humanity became wanderers made for God, but doomed to rebel against Him.

God sent His Son to earth in the form of a baby. Born to a virgin. He lived a sinless life for thirty-three years, when we find it impossible to live without sin for three minutes. He died the death we should have died. He was a perfect substitute, taking the punishment of imperfect

Chapter Ten

people. He then rose from the grave, ascended to heaven with the promise He would bring this invisible heaven to visible earth so we could walk with God in a perfect garden once again.

This gospel is unbelievable! But the only thing more unbelievable is the belief we can spread this message of God without spending time with God! If we abide in Jesus, we will bear much fruit. What then does it take to abide in Jesus?

As I write, my wife and I have been married for twelve years. Before we were married we were high school sweethearts. Before we were high school sweethearts, I was just a guy with a crush on a girl.

I did not think making a connection with her would be easy. She loved basketball, I loved football. She listened to some guy on the radio named Justin Timberlake. My stations never shifted away from R&B. She came from a Caucasian family. My family is the usual Hispanic family, where mama thinks her children can do no wrong, while simultaneously guilt-tripping them about the wrong they have done in order to get what she wants.

Abby's world was not my world, but I wanted to be a part of her world because I liked her, so I attempted to love the things that would connect me with her.

Now, I apologize if this is insensitive, but this was my cross-cultural question in 2004: What do young women love?

In 2004, they loved drinking upside-down caramel macchiatos at Starbucks, while discussing the latest episode of *Friends*. They wanted to walk around Target for hours looking at everything, while not buying anything. They loved watching horrible Matthew McConaughey movies where his shirt accidentally falls off for no apparent reason. Their attention was always diverted by the words, "something-something Old Navy."

Spending extravagant time with her meant having the discipline to love the things that would connect me to her, so I began spending the equivalent of a meal on a cup of coffee from Starbucks. I would walk with her around Target, attempting to be interested in other departments beyond the TV section. I would watch the same Matthew McConaughey movies called by different titles. We would go to Old Navy when they had sales, which was every day.

To love Abby meant learning to love the things that would connect me with Abby. I forced myself to love what she loved on purpose—that is discipline. I then found myself loving what she loved by accident—that is desire. I do enjoy Starbucks now. Matthew McConaughey is making better movies. Old Navy has really comfortable jeans.

Mechanical compliance can lead to an organic choice. Abiding in Jesus can happen the same way. We may not readily feel like spending extravagant time in books or silence, in gatherings or Scripture to get to know Jesus. But, if we choose to love abiding on purpose, we will find ourselves loving to abide by accident.

To borrow the terminology of the Live Dead Missionaries, discipline to abide in Jesus will create desire to abide in Jesus!

This is G. Campbell Morgan, reading a text one hundred times over before he preached it.

This is Fanny Crosby, reciting the four gospels by the time she was ten.

This is Frances Havergal, memorizing all the epistles and the minor prophets, and a small book called Psalm.

This is Martin Luther, praying from 3 a.m. to 6 a.m. because he knew the work of reformation would be great.

This is David Brainerd, having knee indents on his wooden floor from where he would cry out to his God.

This is Jonathan Edwards, reading the Bible by candlelight well into the night, after he put his eleven kids to bed.

This is D.L. Moody, never praying more than five minutes, but never going more than five minutes without praying.

No one inherits a devotional life. We have to build one by insisting devotion should not be limited to a time. Furthermore, we have to

Chapter Ten

remember we are talking about a relationship.

It is possible for love to exist while desire dies!

I began my relationship with my wife by learning to love what she loves to connect with her. Now, we have been married more than ten years.

She will ask, "Will you go to Old Navy with me?"

I will respond, "We do not have money for Old Navy."

She will say, "Let's watch *Downton Abbey* tonight."

I will respond, "But we are watching something else tonight."

She will say, "Will you please get me a glass of water?"

I will respond, "But you are standing closer to the kitchen."

I love her. But, "How can I connect with you?" has become a question requiring discipline to answer. Our relationship began with mechanical compliances becoming organic choices, but over time and through selfishness, organic choices have regressed into mechanical compliances again. We are all familiar with desires we once happily had, easily becoming the disciplines we have to force ourselves to make. Does this mean we are no longer in love? Of course not! It does mean our hearts are prone to choose "me, first" when it comes to each other, and when it comes to Jesus.

Abiding begins with discipline and becomes a delight. But abiding, like anything in life, will not stay there. The desire to abide in Jesus is cyclical. When we find ourselves no longer wanting to be with Jesus through desire, we must force ourselves to choose to be with Jesus through discipline once more.

Our souls are prone to quit. Yet Jesus says, "With God all things are possible" (Matt. 19:26).

"Ask and you will receive. Seek and you will find. Knock and the door will be opened" (Matt. 7:7).

"And I, if I am lifted up from the earth, will draw all peoples to Myself" (John 12:32).

"We do not have a high priest who cannot sympathize with our weaknesses, but was in all points tempted as we are, yet without sin" (Heb. 4:15).

"I will pray the Father, and He will give you another Helper [the Holy Spirit]" (John 14:16).

"Without Me you can do nothing" (John 15:5).

The discipline of abiding precedes the desire for abiding. The desire of abiding will fade, requiring us to take up the discipline of abiding again. Spending extravagant time with Jesus on this side of eternity will be an organic choice and a mechanical compliance.

What, then, is the promise of Jesus to the people who are faithful to abide in Him? He promises we will bear much fruit. Fruit in the Gospel of John has always meant one thing: disciples who make disciples who make disciples.

Is this not how ministry grows? Build discipleship curriculum, but not without abiding in Jesus. Cultivate discipleship culture, but not without abiding in Jesus. Strategize growing small groups, but not without abiding in Jesus. Plan sermons and outreaches, but not without abiding in Jesus. Carefully select the next generation of leaders, but not without abiding in Jesus. Make your marketing worthy of the 21st Century, but not without abiding in Jesus. Grow your leadership skills, but not without abiding in Jesus.

Be methodical, please, but not without abiding in Jesus.

The power of Christendom has always been in the presence of God! Remember John 15:5: "I am the vine, you are the branches. He who abides in Me, and I in him, bears much fruit, for without Me you can do nothing."

So here is the challenge. The Live Dead Missionaries came up with this principle: Abiding is a discipline that leads to a desire that becomes a delight. To practice this principle, they recommend tithing your time to God, giving the Lord the best two hours and twenty-five minutes of your day, every day.

That is extravagant time with Jesus.

Chapter Ten

Will you read the Bible? Will you read books that help you think highly of God? Will you worship? Will you pray for yourself? Will you pray for others? Will you be still and know that He is God? Will you live up to what you now understand?

This is *real* devotion.

Real Devotion

CONCLUSION

BEING A MISSIONARY means calling friends and strangers to ask for a continual investment of money. Sometimes in these phone calls, friends give you more grief than strangers!

I experienced my first call gone bad when I dialed up an old high school friend I had led to the Lord. As soon as I got through my "missionary ask" to be an intern at Sam Houston State Chi Alpha, his response was, "I know about you Chi Alpha guys! I used to support a Chi Alpha missionary in Colorado. (At this point in time, there was no Chi Alpha in Colorado.) All you guys do is go skiing all day while drinking your hot chocolate. (We all drink black coffee.) I am not going to invest in your personal vacation. By the way, get a Chi Alpha started at the University of Texas first. (There was a Chi Alpha already at the University of Texas, around fifteen years old.) Then I will consider investing into you."

After I gave a brief rebuttal to my friend's false facts with real data, I realized that was my first call of the day. I had fifty more to make. I did not pick up my phone again that day. Or the next. Or the next. Or the next.

A full week went by. My budget was at a standstill.

The boy who heard the call of God on a sidewalk on his way to class was a single person responsible only for himself. The man who was rejected on an investment call was a married man responsible for paying rent and feeding his family.

If my money depends on the generosity or monstrosity of humankind, do I want to be a missionary? Now the call of God was not so clear. Now the calling of God was at the mercy of what was convenient. Now what God has asked me to do was being questioned with what my family needs me to do.

Does my soul know that it knows it heard from God?

As I wrestled with quitting the advancement of the gospel, as I was haunted and taunted by a worst-case scenario that has present-tense power to erase future-tense vision, as the sounds of uncertainty became much larger than what I was certain of, I had to stop looking at what I was doing and remember why I was doing it.

I took a walk through campus. During this walk, every place I saw reminded me of an interaction with a person I had found, fed, and fought for.

There was Ross. He was a fraternity guy who could play two-and-a half chords on a guitar. But because he was handsome, every girl asked him for guitar lessons.

There was Kaleb, a big redhead with a kind heart and relative morals. He believed in reading the Bible. He also believed in drinking before the age of twenty-one.

There was Edgard, a Hispanic Romeo who just had his heart broken from a previous relationship. We had a habit of listening to sad songs in an effort to embrace grief to overcome grief. Soon he met Jesus and his sad heart became whole.

There was Josh. He was a gamer who excelled at anything with buttons. The key to his heart was video game nights every Friday from midnight until 6 a.m. the following morning. He wrestled with the rationality of a good God allowing bad things.

There was Brian, a baseball player who kept to himself, but the right momma joke at the right time could turn the biggest introvert into the greatest extrovert you have ever seen.

There was Little John. He enjoyed wearing plain white tees while listening to the band, "Plain White T's." We never let him forget this. He committed his life to Jesus in a way he would never forget. He is not so little anymore.

Of these six guys, five gave their lives to Jesus. One has continued to doubt. There is still opportunity because there is still breath in his lungs.

Watching these guys transform from rebels into worshipers was something that transformed me. When Ross gave his life to Jesus, he read the New Testament in two weeks and the Old Testament in three weeks. His roommates could overhear him crying out to God for their own souls.

When Edgard gave his life to Jesus, his integration point moved away from a girl in his life to the God of the universe. He then went out on mission to love the unlovable and remember the forgotten of our campus.

When Brian gave his life to Jesus, he became a missionary to Kazakhstan and then to Chile. This introvert could not help telling people about Jesus.

After Kaleb gave his life to Jesus, he went into the marketplace. He is salt and light in his office. He also voluntarily serves as his church's youth pastor.

After John gave his life to Jesus, he went into the marketplace, but not before giving every summer in college to overseas missions. Now he gives all his money to missions while making disciples with his church.

They love God. They hate sin. They pray for people continually. They read the Bible day and night. They made disciples without the title of small group leader. They went on to make disciples with the title of small group leader.

As this walk continued, I saw all the places on campus where I had become closer to Jesus. There was the spot my small group leader told me to make Jesus the integration point of my life, not because of what He does, but because of who He is.

There was the library where I read about sin not breaking impersonal laws but the personal heart of God.

There was the computer lab where spontaneous conversations would be focused on how God's laws are not motivations for obedience, but descriptions of reality.

There was the sidewalk where I had walked slowly away from class, listening and being changed by a sermon that said, "May the Lamb who was slain receive the reward of His suffering."[23]

There was the apartment complex. Inside its doors is the living room where I gave my life to Jesus and told Him to never let me ask for it back. He has been good to the deal.

I then found myself back home, entering round twelve with the same question: If my money depends on the generosity or monstrosity of humankind, do I want to be a missionary? Now the call of God was clear. Now the calling of God required commitment over convenience. Now what God has asked me to do could be done while fulfilling what my family needed me to do.

My soul knew that it knew it had heard from God! I was occupied with "whats." I needed to remember my "why." When I discovered the why again, the rest was history.

I will say it again: What Christians do will never be real if it is disconnected from the revelation and awe of why we do it.

Whether you are trying to be a disciple or make a disciple, life can offer much to disconnect us from the revelation and awe of Jesus. Promotions and finite glory can corrupt motive. God's laws conflicting with our desires can silence sobriety. Enjoying sin can weaken the reality

Conclusion

that sin breaks God's heart. We do not want God to have a right on our life when we want to do wrong. Meeting needs can cost us something we do not want to pay. A sober sense of reality can sting before it saves. Self-denial is the odd-man out in a world of self-absorption. Prayer and time are at odds. Success and suffering have produced many casualties in and out of Christian service. The cyclical nature of abiding requires trusting entirely in God and nothing in self.

There is much that can disconnect us from Jesus. This is why the secret to being a disciple and making disciples hinges on making the "whys" of the gospel familiar to our souls.

Let us make disciples. That is *fruit*.

Let us be disciples. That is *abiding*.

Let us fulfill the "whats" of the gospel. That is *devotion*.

Let us be fully convicted of the "whys" of the gospel. That is *real devotion*.

FOOTNOTES

Introduction

1   FW Boreham, *My Christmas Book* (John Broadbanks Publishing, 2015), p. 84

2   From the *2019 Discipleship Pathway Assessment*, a study by Lifeway Research

3   From the Barna Group: *State of the Church 2020*

Motive is, "Why Do You Do the Things You Do and Who You Do Them For?"

4   Tim Keller, *The Prodigal God* (Penguin Books, 2016) p. 46. God's laws are not motivations for obedience but descriptions of reality from an infinite perspective.

5   Winkie Pratney, "God's Right is Founded in His Value" (lecture, 21st Century Reformation Conference, New Zealand, May 2005). Sin is not the breaking of impersonal law, but of the personal heart of God

6   This dialogue is based on a sermon illustration by Eli Stewart from Chi Alpha Campus Ministries, USA

7   C.S. Lewis, *The Four Loves* (Harcourt Brace Jovanovich Publishers, 1960), p. 169

8   George Otis Jr, *The God They Never Knew* (Mott Media Inc, 1982), p. 208

God Has a Right to Our Life Not Because of What He Does, But Who He Is

9   J. Robert Clinton, "Finishing Well: Six Characteristics."

10 E. Stanley Jones, *The Christ on the Indian Road* (Grosset & Dunlap, 1925)

11 Winkie Pratney, "God's Right is Founded in His Value" (lecture, 21st Century Reformation Conference, New Zealand, May 2005) Love is unselfishly choosing for the highest good of God and His Kingdom

12 This quote is from Mother Theresa, founder of Missionaries of Charity, Kolkata, India

13 Dick Brogden, *This Gospel* (Live Dead Publishing, 2018)

14 C.S. Lewis, *Mere Christianity* (Harper Collins, 2001), p. 215

15 Malcolm Muggeridge, *Jesus the Man Who Lives* (Fontana, 1975), p. 16

Humility is a Sober Sense of Reality

17 Tim Keller, "Pride: The Case of Nebuchadnezzar" (lecture, Redeemer Church, New York, February 1995)

18 This quote is from Philip Brooks, most known for rector of Trinity Church, Boston, Massachusetts

19 Deitrich Bonhoeffer, *Life Together* (Harper Collins, 1954), p. 96, 97

Prayer is Not About What You Do, But Whose You Are
20 Tim Keller, "Basis of Prayer: Our Father" (lecture, Redeemer Church, New York, April 1995)

21 This dialogue is based on a sermon illustration Dick Foth from Penguin Random House, and National Community Church, Washington, D.C.

Discipline, Desire, Delight
22 William Barclay, *The Gospel of John, Volume 2* (The Westminster Press Philadelphia, 1956), p. 202

Conclusion
23 From a sermon by Paris Reidhead, "Ten Shekels and a Shirt," where he references the Moravian Missionary statement.